DATE DUE

NOV 0 4 1994		
MAR 1 8 1996		
MAY 0 1 1997		

HIGHSMITH 45-220

PRAIRIE
The Land and Its People

c.1

Text and Photography
Mil Penner and Carol Schmidt

Foreword
Senator Nancy Landon Kassebaum

Design
Liz King

Publisher
The Sounds of Kansas
Inman, Kansas

PRAIRIE is dedicated to the wind that carries the fragrance of the wild prairie rose and the meadowlark's song; to the vast sky that brings the rain; to the rich earth that holds the deep-rooted grasses; and to everyone who feels the immanency of the land. Our hope is that children of the earth may enjoy the prairie's blessings forever.

Copyright © 1989
by Sounds of Kansas.
All rights reserved.
Published 1990.
Printed in the
United States of America.

Direct all inquiries to:
Sounds of Kansas
Route 1
Inman, Kansas   67546
316.585.2389

Project Coordinator:
Ken Quimby

Design and Production:
Liz King Design

Editor:
Mary Campbell Nielsen

Typesetting:
Impressions, Inc.

Separations and Printing:
Sun Graphics Inc.

Library of Congress
Number 89-91644

ISBN: 0-9615597-1-3

III. Reflections

Timeline
Present Time

— *Mammals*
— *Dinosaurs*
— *Coal Swamps*
— *Fish*
— *Land Plants*

— *Spores*

1 Billion Years Ago

— *Advanced Cells*

2 Billion Years Ago

3 Billion Years Ago

— *Primitive Cells*

4 Billion Years Ago

— *Solar System Formed*

5 Billion Years Ago

AMERICAN PRAIRIE

SOUTH AMERICAN PAMPAS

AFRICA

Major Grasslands

American Prairie
South American Pampas
African Veldt
European Steppes
Australian Lowlands

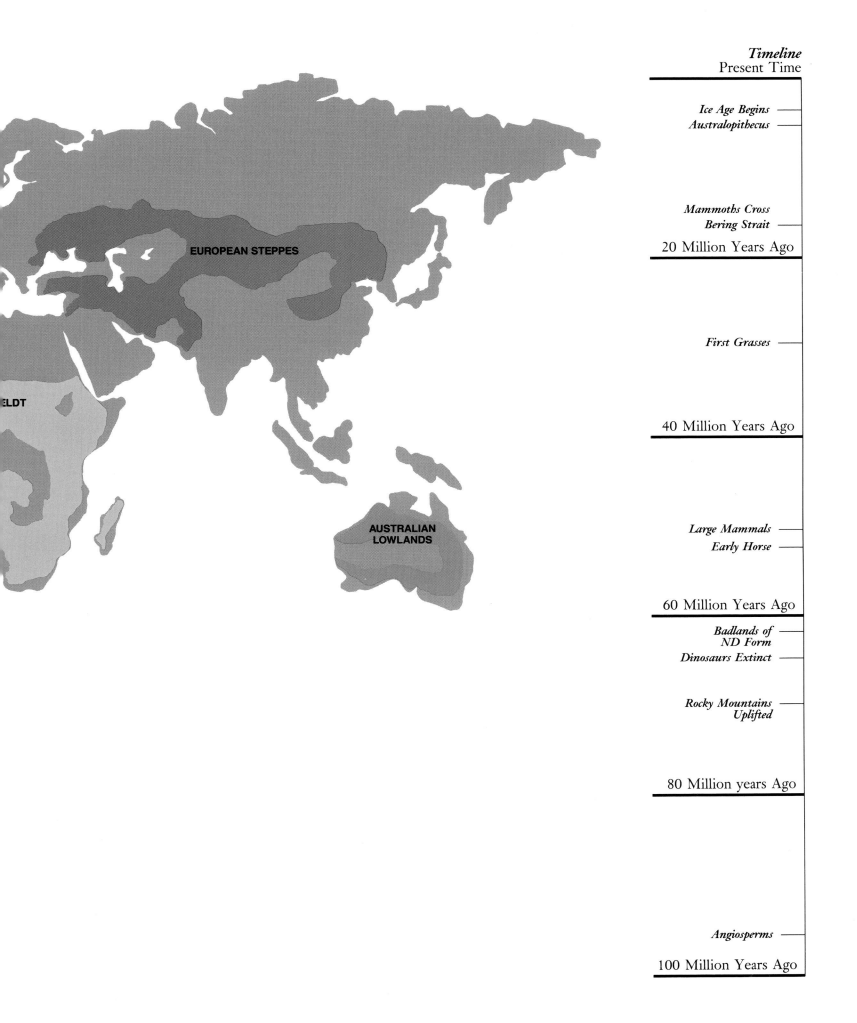

EUROPEAN STEPPES

ELDT

AUSTRALIAN LOWLANDS

Timeline
Present Time

Ice Age Begins
Australopithecus

Mammoths Cross
Bering Strait
20 Million Years Ago

First Grasses

40 Million Years Ago

Large Mammals
Early Horse

60 Million Years Ago
Badlands of
ND Form
Dinosaurs Extinct

Rocky Mountains
Uplifted

80 Million years Ago

Angiosperms
100 Million Years Ago

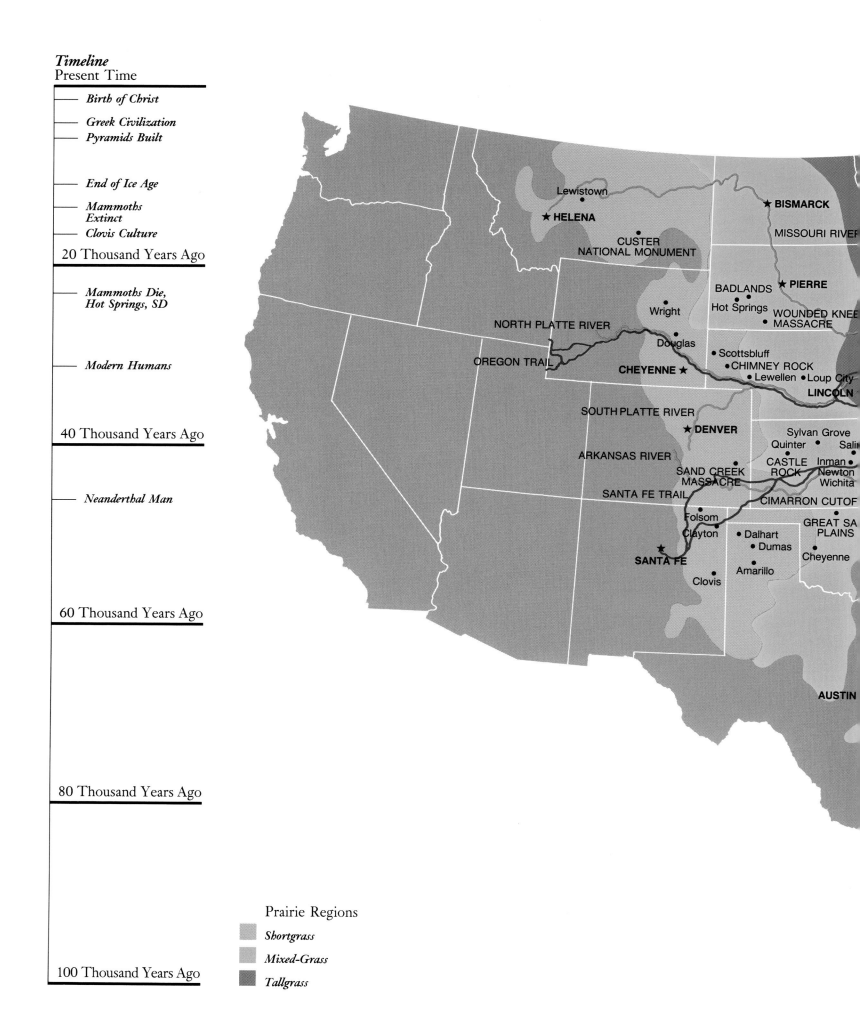

Timeline
Present Time

— *Birth of Christ*

— *Greek Civilization*
— *Pyramids Built*

— *End of Ice Age*

— *Mammoths Extinct*
— *Clovis Culture*

20 Thousand Years Ago

— *Mammoths Die, Hot Springs, SD*

— *Modern Humans*

40 Thousand Years Ago

— *Neanderthal Man*

60 Thousand Years Ago

80 Thousand Years Ago

100 Thousand Years Ago

Prairie Regions

Shortgrass

Mixed-Grass

Tallgrass

Lewistown
★ HELENA
CUSTER
NATIONAL MONUMENT
★ BISMARCK
MISSOURI RIVER
BADLANDS ★ PIERRE
Hot Springs
WOUNDED KNEE
MASSACRE
Wright
NORTH PLATTE RIVER
Douglas
OREGON TRAIL
Scottsbluff
CHIMNEY ROCK
Lewellen ● Loup City
CHEYENNE ★
LINCOLN
SOUTH PLATTE RIVER
★ DENVER
Sylvan Grove
Quinter ● Salin
ARKANSAS RIVER
CASTLE Inman ●
ROCK Newton
SAND CREEK Wichita
MASSACRE
SANTA FE TRAIL
CIMARRON CUTOF
Folsom
GREAT SA
PLAINS
Clayton
● Dalhart
● Dumas
Cheyenne
SANTA FE
Amarillo
Clovis

AUSTIN

Timeline

Present Time

Space Age

Aldo Leopold

Atomic Age

First Airplane

Wounded Knee Massacre

100 Years Ago

Transcontinental Railroad

Indian Wars

Civil War

Walden Pond Written

Oregon Trail

Santa Fe Trail

Louisiana Purchase

200 Years Ago

United States Independence

300 Years Ago

Pilgrims Land

400 Years Ago

DeSoto Discovers Mississippi

Coronado's Expedition

Cortez Invades Mexico

500 Years Ago

LAKE SUPERIOR

LAKE HURON

LAKE MICHIGAN

LAKE ONTARIO

LAKE ERIE

MISSISSIPPI RIVER

ST. PAUL ★

• Sanborn

Pipestone

North Freedom • Baraboo

• LANSING ★

★ MADISON

Marion •

Chicago •

• Grand Detour

DES MOINES ★

Moline •

INDIANAPOLIS ★

Toledo •

Paulding •

COLUMBUS ★

★ SPRINGFIELD

• Terre Haute

Saverton •

St. Louis •

★ PEKA

JEFFERSON CITY ★

Charleston •

Fairdealing •

LAHOMA CITY

• LAKE WISTER

Wolfe City •

From the front porch of my home in the Kansas Flint Hills, I look out across a sea of rolling hills cloaked in the rich, deep green of spring or the crackling gray-brown of winter. The vast blue sky forms a canopy over a land that rests at peace, the silence broken only by the rustle of grass or the song of meadowlarks.

I come here as often as I can, though never often enough. I walk across the fields or sit and read in the quiet of a place that is truly home. Most of all, I regain a sense of timelessness, of connection to the earth and so to things that are genuinely fundamental.

Prairie: The Land and Its People offers poignant testimony to the beauty, the joy, and the great affection of people who live and work and travel in these lands. The photographs and vignettes of this book tell a remarkable story, one that comes from the heart and touches the heart.

Prairie is a special book about very special places and I commend it to all who turn its pages. Even more than that, I commend to you its subject—the prairie—and urge you to go there and witness firsthand the happy marriage of earth and sky. Then you may begin to understand what is meant by the word "reverence."

—Senator Nancy Landon Kassebaum

PRAIRIE
The Land and Its People

Introduction: Natural Prairie

To appreciate the prairie land is to touch the bare bones of prehistory, to walk in the weathered tracks of covered wagons, to hear the meadowlark, and to see a clear stream of life-giving water. Today the prairie land is covered with fields of corn, grazing cattle, ribbons of concrete and steel, houses, and skyscrapers. Still, the essential element necessary to sustain life is the endless prairie cycle of earth, air, and water converting the sun's energy to food and fiber.

Carol and I had set out to capture the awesome drama of the prairie lands, but we soon learned that it was we who were captive . . . to the spirit, vibrancy, and beauty of the land and its denizens . . . people and all other creatures great and small.

I have always loved to work with the earth and the things that grow. I have plowed the soil, planted seeds and watched them flourish. I have experienced the power of subduing the earth with huge machines and chemical wonders. I have transformed wetlands, grasslands, and woodlands into productive, lucrative farmland. But finally, I began to have questions.

Determined to find the balance between progress and preservation, Carol and I began our prairie journeys. We met the spring in Texas, Oklahoma, and New Mexico, thrilled by a profusion of roadside flowers, blooming redbuds, and air as clear as glass. We followed the Oregon Trail along the Platte Valley in Nebraska and Wyoming, wondering why settlers chose to go beyond this land of sandhill cranes and breath-taking wide-open spaces. In Iowa, Illinois, Indiana, and Ohio we found prairie relicts amid thriving cities and lush fields of corn.

Enchanting prairie grasses and flowers met us from the mountains of Colorado to the forests of Missouri, Michigan, and Wisconsin. Crossing the Missouri River by ferry in the rugged Montana Missouri Breaks, we continued our adventure downstream along the Lewis and Clark Trail through the Mandan Indian region of North Dakota, into South Dakota where steamboats used to churn the river with their paddle wheels. Minnesota offered precious traces of history in Indian petroglyphs and a sod house. Still, for us the prairie land is at its best in our beloved Kansas in May, when fields of wheat wave in the wind and flowers are resplendent in the Flint Hills.

There is a spirit in the prairie land that touches me deeply. There is a truth, almost tangible, reaching out from the earth itself through nature. The short vignettes that follow depict a personal encounter with that truth in the prairie land of the United States.

Mil Penner

Left: Indian grass with pitcher sage.

Alyssa

Holding little Alyssa, our first grandchild, in my arms the first day of her life touched me deeply. Her beauty, her completeness, and even her clamorous demands for the nourishment and love she needed spoke of the wonder of life's natural processes. Her hands, tiny replicas of my scarred ones, beat the air, and her feet thumped against my stomach, telling me she was not where she wanted to be. As I embraced this new life, strong and vigorous, fragile and innocent, I felt both joy and responsibility.

The joy was for my children, Murray and Nadine, with the adventure of parenthood ahead of them; as well as for V. Lee, my wife, whose eyes glistened as she held the baby. I imagined some future day when this little girl would come to our farm. I would take her hand and show her the world we live in, walking with her in our own little prairie, picking delicate purple prairie clover and lifting her up to peek at baby mourning doves in their precarious pine-tree nest.

The overwhelming feeling of responsibility came when I sensed the trust she already seemed to place in me, in the moments when she rested serenely in my arms and looked at me with eyes that seemed to say, "I trust you, Grandpa. You have made a good world for me to come into."

When Alyssa's father was a young boy, part of our farm, which we called the pasture, was unbroken sod. True, the native buffalo grass was heavily overgrazed, with wire-grass and thistles threatening, but the buffalo wallows still imprinted on the land were proof of the pasture's virginity. Murray used to run his heart out, following the sheep paths to the far corners, while his grandmother, still living on the farm, would worry about the buck "getting him."

Whether or not the foot-deep water holes we called buffalo wallows were really made by the bison is arguable. In any event, the depressions were the last vestiges of the unbroken prairie. The sheep trails, fanning out from a little bridge over the creek, represented the days when small farms dotted the land and cattle or sheep marched out in single file from the lot near the barn every morning to graze.

Purple prairie clover and other prairie flowers are known as forbs: non-woody flowering plants other than grasses. Like other legumes, purple prairie clover can convert atmospheric nitrogen into available nitrogen in the soil via nodules on the roots that contain nitrogen-fixing bacteria.

Buffalo wallows were formed by bison rolling in the dirt, coating themselves with dust to eliminate parasites. During rainy seasons these holes filled with water, providing food resources for shore birds. These wallows have been eliminated on cultivated land.

*Left: Alyssa Penner.
Above: Purple prairie clover.*

Now, with Alyssa on my lap, I recalled with sadness how I, as a young farmer in the late fifties, decided to plow the pasture because someone had said we would make more money growing wheat than raising sheep. I'll never forget driving into the pasture with the old Farmall "M" tractor and a three-bottom plow, while Murray, seven years old, tears streaming down his face, ran his trails for the last time.

Thinking about the old days brought to mind stories my dad had told me about the thousands of ducks and geese that used to stop every fall and spring in the shallow lakes and swamps north of our farm. In the late 1800's, before Grandfather and his neighbors drained the land, this area had been a hunter's paradise.

Driving home from our first visit with Alyssa, V. Lee and I discussed the importance of preserving such natural treasures for our granddaughter. Last spring, I witnessed a flock of Canada geese flying so low that I could hear the soft stroking of their wings as these avian migrants disappeared into the gently falling snow. The magic of their honking conversation in the pristine snow is a legacy I want to leave for Alyssa.

Changes in agriculture, dictated by economics and technology, leave their mark on the land. Early prairie-state farms tended to be small and diversified. Most farms had a pasture, a hay field, mixed crops, a variety of livestock, and possibly an orchard. Such diversity provided a broader environmental basis for wildlife than does today's monocultural orientation.

Large farm machinery makes small fields impractical, thus eliminating many fence rows which harbored wildlife. Modern equipment makes leveling and draining the land economically feasible, while economic pressures on the farmer promote more aggressive land usage.

Left: White eveningprimrose. Above: Canada geese, NE.

The Badlands

Among phantasmal twisted canyons and towers of white crumbling rock, the third day of Creation continues. Raw parent materials, the stuff earth is made of, fall from naked pinnacles eroded out of the Dakota plains on their way to becoming topsoil somewhere downstream. Extremes of temperature, wind, and water rip this land into grotesque shapes. This fearsome place is called the South Dakota Badlands.

Leaving Interstate 90, we approached the Badlands from the north, driving on a level high plain made up of ancient drift materials from the Rocky Mountains. It was bitterly cold when we arrived and first saw what appeared to be a mountain range viewed from the top, with irregular valleys cut into the land hundreds of feet deep. From our vantage point it was obvious that the Badlands were eroding northward into the plains, like a waterfall moving back into its rocky bed.

The formations left standing displayed beautiful multicolored strata exposing sixty-five million years of changes. Within these layers are fossils dating back to the formation's development. On the lower level, once the bottom of an ocean, little fossil ammonites are found. Larger fossils of alligators and elephant-like creatures appear in higher strata.

A government soil conservationist once told me that it takes nature thousands of years to produce one inch of topsoil. At the time, it was hard to comprehend. Here, looking down on the tortuous landscape, the conservationist's words came back to me, and I understood. The process of building soil was occurring right in front of us.

The development of a particular handful of topsoil may have begun when frost cracked a boulder from a mountain peak in the Rockies. The rock broke up as it tumbled, and some pieces fell into a river, disintegrating as swift water dashed them into other rocks. Granules arriving years later at the Badlands, combining with sediment from the dried-up ocean floor, supported some primitive grasses. When the grass died, part of the root residue attached itself to this clod of dirt. More debris came along and covered it up.

All prairie soils are derived from parent rock. Frost, water, wind, and glaciers break up rock into fine particles to form the basis of soil. In the course of this process, soils from different sources are mixed and distributed over wide areas. Topsoil is produced from the pulverized parent rock by the interaction of weather, the topography, and the plants, animals, and microorganisms of a region over time.

The prairie grasses and forbs were dominant forces in building the rich prairie soils which today are called the breadbasket of the country. The total ecological balance of the prairie contributed to this effort. When this balance is disturbed, soil-building ceases.

The monocultures of corn, wheat, sorghum, and other crops do not produce topsoil. In fact, they deplete the soil unless nutrients, in the form of fertilizers, are added. The agricultural practices associated with these crops stifle the animals, insects, and microorganisms necessary to build soil.

Left: The Badlands, SD.
Above: Cascade Falls, SD.

Millenia later, this clod, exposed by erosion, is precariously attached to a vulnerable clay spire. A bird's talon sends it falling to the plain. As rainwater moves it downstream, it mixes with other soils, which combine all their nutrients and provide the seedbed for a golden pea. Some nearby bacteria attach themselves to this legume, adding nitrogen to the clump of earth. Slowly the mixing and assimilating continue.

The prairie grasses and forbs on the watersheds below the Badlands finish the process of making topsoil. Deep roots open the soils, and then a host of prairie residents—fungi, bacteria, worms, animals, and more—eat and digest the roots and grasses to make humus.

A particular grain of soil can end up almost anywhere. A whirlwind may pick it up and carry it to Minnesota, or rain may wash it down the White River into the Missouri and finally into the Mississippi Delta.

Prairie dogs and coyotes dig their dens on the plain below the Badlands, unaware that their digging, eating, killing, and dying are part of a birthing process.

Topsoil, essential to life, is being depleted at an alarming rate. Good conservation practices in effect today help to arrest the depletion. Topsoil is a replenishable resource, but an ecologically complete prairie system functioning over a long period of time is necessary to sustain it. Research, on a limited scale, is in progress to develop a self-sustaining form of agriculture, one which would maintain the soil's quality.

Left: Buffalo grass.
Above: Prairie dog.

War: Forest and Prairie

There was a forest stalking westward through dwarfed prairie grasses. Hickory, aspen, maple, and oak, limbs straining forward, pushed the grasses aside like football players crunching through a weaker team. Abundant sunshine, rain-bearing clouds, and cooling ocean breezes cheered the wooden soldiers on. The trees had grown profusely in the luxuriant land, spending nutrients lavishly on trunks, branches, and masses of leaves. The woodlands were crowded. It was time for war, forest against prairie, but the conflict appeared very one-sided.

Vainly the grasses fought back, seeking to hold their ground. Timing their resistance to the rhythm of the wind, the grasses would lean back, then in undulating waves sweep up against the forest's leading edge of wild plum, grape, dogwood, and sumac. Stronger and fiercer winds would propel the grasses again and again; the huge trees would shake down their leaves in disdain and advance once more. The forest's victory seemed imminent.

Far to the west was a contrasting drama. In the shadow of great rising mountains, amid the glow of volcanic explosions and storms of fire, between fingers of molten lava, the prairie was maturing. An evolutionary cycle of erosion and dying grasses was creating new soil, from which in turn stronger grasses and flowers emerged. The sky above offered the sun's blazing energy and very little rain.

The grasses and forbs learned hard lessons in the west. They became very frugal with moisture and hoarded most nutrients and life forces underground. They adapted to the wind, bending gracefully, springing back after each onslaught. Animals grazed them to the ground, and they sent up new shoots from the base. In wintertime they retreated into the earth, forgoing the vanity of great bulk.

Conspiring with the prairie flora against the advancing forest, the mountains held back the Pacific rain clouds. The sun parched the land, shriveling the vulnerable leaves of the forest's western troops, while the grasses called upon their deep reserves. Cyclones joined the fray, lashing out cruelly at the land to the advantage of the resilient grasses as trees crashed and broke. Raging blizzards and heavy ice pulled limb from limb and trunk, as Arctic cold tested the forest's mettle while the grasses and forbs rested in the warmer earth.

Throughout time no fixed boundaries have divided prairie and forest. Geological events, such as the ice ages, and climatic variances determine prairie limits. Present prairie grasslands developed twenty-five million years ago after the Rocky Mountains emerged, restricting the moisture flow from the Pacific Ocean.

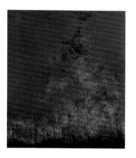

Prairie rainfall annual averages range from ten inches in the west to thirty-nine inches in the eastern prairie extremes. Grasses and forbs are more adapted to dry, windy climates than are trees and shrubs.

About half of a full-grown grass plant's material is underground. In a forest, only ten percent of the biomass is under the surface. The extra underground reserve makes grasses and forbs more tolerant than trees of drought, grazing, mowing, and fire.

Left: Ted Shank Wildlife Refuge, MO. Above: Prairie fire.

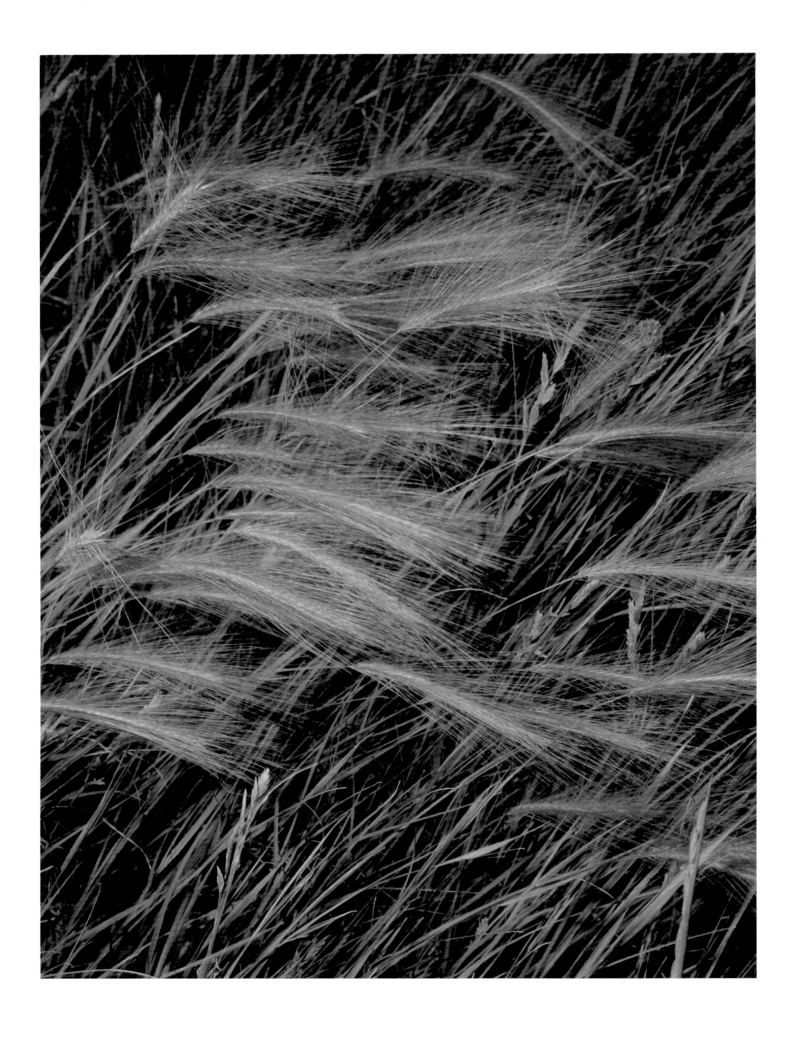

The forest faltered, but it was not defeated. The trees, too, learned to adapt to adversity, sending out the stronger, more deeply rooted oaks to do battle. Squirrels burying acorns a few yards farther west each year moved the lowly bur oaks into the prairie's heartland, but the hot summer sun stopped them there.

The prairie had one more powerful weapon, fire, which it held back until the snows melted. The mountains cunningly sent the pent cloud energy eastward to replenish the prairies. The capricious clouds released bolts of fire to set the grasslands ablaze before the rains fell. The fires consumed the dead grasses and forbs and the living small trees invading the prairie land. Then the rains of spring followed, and the green shoots of grasses and forbs came out of winter hiding places.

I awoke with a start as a clap of thunder rolled across the sky and rain began to pelt my window. My book, explaining the balance of forest and prairie, had dropped to the floor. Outside, branches crashed to the ground as the spring storm raged. A nearby field of wheat, distant cousin to vanquished prairie, was unable to absorb the dashing rain.

Grasses, if mowed, grazed, or burned, grow new shoots from the base. Most woody plants die if clipped or burned. Prairie wildfires prevented the growth of woody plants in the eastern grassland regions. Burning of grasslands is considered an acceptable maintenance practice today.

Plowing and the absence of free-ranging fires have made abandoned farmland in the eastern prairie susceptible to forest encroachment. Forests are vital to the global ecological balance of oxygen and carbon dioxide.

Left: Foxtail barley.
Above: Oak, elm, and maple leaves.

Folsom

Folsom, New Mexico, died years ago, probably in 1908. A few people live there anyway, and I envy them. Folsom is the refreshing antithesis of modern efficiency. Prairie meets mountain and culture meets culture in structures of adobe, quarried rock, and red cedar. The town resonates with the charm of the Old West and the mystery of Eden.

Bears meander into town occasionally, credit cards are not accepted, and men have been known to ride their horses up to the bar in the local tavern. Visitors to the little museum learn of posses chasing train robbers and of heroic Sarah Rooke, a telephone operator, who in 1908 stayed at her post to warn townspeople of the onrushing water until the flood swept her to her death.

The Cimarron River flood, which almost annihilated Folsom, started a chain of discoveries that should be recorded in every American-history book. The first evidence of an American culture at least ten thousand years old was discovered in Wild Horse Arroyo, eight miles west of town. George McJunkin, a self-educated black cowboy, discovered bones protruding from a bank eroded by flood waters. From his experience as a buffalo hunter, McJunkin realized that these were not ordinary bones, but he did not live long enough to learn the full impact of his discovery.

Almost twenty years later, excavations at the site revealed a spear point embedded in the rib cage of a huge bison of a type that has been extinct for over ten thousand years. This evidence linking ice-age animals with primitive hunters, identified as "Folsom Man," is now on display in the Denver Museum of Natural History. Later archaeological explorers in the Southwest, near Clovis, New Mexico, discovered an even earlier culture, which they called "Clovis Man." The Clovis people were contemporaneous with the mammoth, which they hunted for food. The mammoth was extinct by nine thousand B.C., before the Folsom period.

The Clovis and Folsom cultures apparently originated in Asia and crossed over what is now Bering Strait on a narrow land bridge about twelve thousand years ago. They were capable of making tools and clothing and may have developed a throwing stick, or atlatl, to hurl spears through tough animal hides.

The development of the Clovis and Folsom cultures occurred during a period of great change in the prairie. The Wisconsin Glacier, the last ice-age glacier, was in retreat, and Capulin Mountain, the last active volcano in the area, became dormant.

Ten thousand years ago most of the large mammals had become extinct. Up to that time Columbian mammoths, giant bison antiquus, *camels, horses, and short-faced bears lived on the plains. The grasses were taller than those of today, and there were more trees.*

Left: Mt. Capulin, extinct volcano, NM. Above: Folsom livery, NM.

Long before the ice age, featherless flying pterodactyls and eighty-foot dinosaurs weighing thirty-five tons inhabited the Folsom region as well as the rest of the North American continent two hundred million to sixty-five million years ago. At that time the Gulf of Mexico's shores were near present-day Clayton, New Mexico. In Clayton Lake State Park, tracks made by dinosaurs are visible in thin layers of Dakota sandstone unearthed during construction of a spillway. Sixty-five million years ago the dinosaurs mysteriously disappeared. After the age of the dinosaurs, the ancestral grasses and flowers appeared, the Rocky Mountains began their violent accretion, and mammals started their sluggish evolution.

When the sun sets behind the mountains west of Folsom, a few clouds diffusing light into fiery glow, it is easy to envision a night ten thousand years ago when nearby Capulin Mountain shot fire, ashes, and lava into the sky. It must have terrified the people of the Folsom culture, sitting around campfires, maybe watching the night sky explode and thinking about the next day's hunt of the giant Pleistocene bison.

Folsom is not dead after all. It has been alive for thousands of years, and it still nourishes the green grasses, the orange Indian paintbrush, and a few people so trustworthy that there are no locks on the doors.

Two theories exist about the extinction of the large mammals. One suggests that environmental change, such as grass becoming shorter and less plentiful, was responsible. Another idea is that early man hunted and destroyed them. The horse, ironically, evolved on the American continent, crossed the land bridge to Asia, and developed there to its present form. Horses returned with the Spanish conquistadors to the Americas where the species had become extinct.

Left: Sunset, Folsom, NM. Above: View from Mt. Capulin, NM; Indian paintbrush.

Palmer's Cave

There is a place in the unplowed, mixed-grass prairie range land of Ellsworth County, Kansas, where history is tangible but the enigma of the unknown is more pressing. West of Salina and south of Interstate 70, beyond the din of traffic, vultures soar on heat thermals, just as they always have, and Mulberry Creek cuts a little deeper into the red sandstone every year. Here Palmer's Cave and the nearby countryside are a crossroads of geography, time, history, and the unknown.

Not many miles away stand steel towers with huge wheels and cables that lower men into a salt bed laid down epochs ago by a prehistoric ocean. Close by are an abandoned nineteenth-century sheep ranch with stone fences, ruts of the Butterfield Trail, and eerie cairns standing like Old-Testament sacrificial altars on the hilltops.

These cairns, stone piled on stone, rise bleakly from distant high points. Who built them? What was their purpose? No one knows. The few people who live nearby simply say, "The cairns have always been here." Which of the many cultures that have occupied this land erected them? Wichita and Pawnee Indian boundaries met here, John C. Fremont explored here, the Pawnee and Butterfield trails and the Fort Harker Military Road crossed the land, and Basque shepherds guarded flocks before waves of settlers arrived. All left their influence at this place. The riddle of these rocks, placed here so carefully many years ago, remains.

In a nearby valley, we were guided to Palmer's cave by anthropology student Annette White. She led us along a path she had hacked out of stinging nettles and poison ivy a few days earlier. As we climbed she told us the story of a tragic massacre here.

Overlooking Mulberry Creek, the cave has been sculpted out of a sandstone cliff by time and the elements. The entrance, low enough to make a visitor crawl, led into a small chamber with enough dim light to reveal Indian petroglyphs carved into the wall. Vying for space on the wall were scratched initials and dates from 1860 to the present. An opening like a picture window let in some sunlight but was almost inaccessible from the outside because of the steep slope. "It's too cool for the rat snakes and spiders to be out," Ms. White said.

The mixed-grass prairie occurs in north-central Texas, central Oklahoma, Kansas, and Nebraska, and most of the Dakotas. Since the mixed-grass prairie is a transitional zone between the tallgrass prairie and the shortgrass prairie, there are no fixed boundaries. High rainfall periods will move tall grasses such as big bluestem westward. Low rainfall will bring buffalo and the grama grasses east. Annual rainfall ranges from fourteen to twenty-three inches.

Warm-season little bluestem shares dominance with cool-season June grass and need-legrasses. In the north, cool-season western wheatgrass may dominate. Cool-season grasses thrive in the spring, produce seed, and are dormant in the summer, often greening again in wet early fall seasons. Warm-season grasses green up later but grow all summer, produce seed in the late summer, and then become dormant.

The mixed-grass prairie region is our country's major wheat and grain sorghum source. Corn and soybeans are produced where irrigation water is available.

Left: Buckbrush and little bluestem. Above: Cairn, Ellsworth Co., KS.

Outside, from a boggy vantage point below the window, more petroglyphs were visible in the stone, depicting bison, tepees, and numinous symbols. One large, reclining figure appeared to be a dying chief and a message of impending doom, possibly smallpox, for the tribe. Recent bullet holes obscured some of the sacred marks.

The massacre story is that a troop of cavalrymen from Fort Harker and one of the pioneer ranchers came across a group of Pawnees. The rancher asked the troopers to kill the Indians. They refused, saying that they were forbidden to initiate hostilities. The rancher resolved that; he shot a warrior in the back. During the ensuing battle, the Pawnees sought safety in Palmer's Cave.

The rancher left, returning with a wagon full of dry hay. He maneuvered it to one of the cave entrances and set it afire. As the suffocating braves plunged out of the south entrance above the creek, the soldiers shot them.

More than 120 winters after that shameful day, petroglyphs carved into red rock and weathered cairns still speak metaphorically for people who loved life and nature and who contemplated the mysteries of God.

On these windswept prairie hillsides, landmarks and symbols provide but a crude framework for speculation about the unknown.

American Indian populations in the forty-eight states declined from above five million at the time of Columbus to about 250 thousand at the turn of the twentieth century. Disease, whiskey, displacement, and genocide, all resulting from white emigration, were responsible.

Left: Goldenrod spider and cabbage white butterfly. Above: Palmer's Cave, KS.

Trails and Rails

In a remote little cemetery overlooking the Mississippi River stands a weathered tombstone bearing the dates 1799 and 1901. The name, almost illegible, appears to be John. The life span, touching as it does three centuries, is intriguing, but the concurrent history of the prairie lands between the Mississippi River and the Rocky Mountains is even more astounding. During John's lifetime, this wild country became the heartland of America, the breadbasket of the world, and a teeming center of commerce.

President Thomas Jefferson acquired the Louisiana Territory, comprising most of the prairie land west of the Mississippi, when John was four years old. The next year Lewis and Clark started their epic journey, exploring the territory and the Columbia River. A few years later Zebulon Pike reported that the western half of the territory was desert, unfit for human habitation.

In John's twenty-second year, William Becknell made the first pack-mule-train journey to the Spanish city of Santa Fe. The Erie Canal, joining the Atlantic Ocean and Lake Erie, opened in 1825, and construction began on other canals linking the Ohio River with Lake Erie through Ohio and Indiana.

In John's thirty-first year the Tom Thumb, America's first coal-burning steam locomotive, made its initial run in Baltimore. It doomed the Ohio River-Lake Erie canals before their completion, and germinated the potential empire in the west. Four years later, Chicago was incorporated as a town. In the late 1830's, the eastern prairie grasses in Illinois, Indiana, and Wisconsin were being plowed with Deere's new polished-steel walking plow.

The fifth decade of John's life saw the Oregon Trail develop along the Platte River valley. More than eighteen thousand pioneers—Oregon-bound settlers and Mormons going to Utah—used this route before the California gold rush began in 1849. For these emigrants, the prairie was the most desolate part of the journey. They looked forward to the sight of Chimney Rock, harbinger of less monotonous scenery, in western Nebraska. Precarious Mitchell Pass, two days beyond Chimney Rock, often replaced their prairie boredom with anxiety.

Captain Meriwether Lewis, President Jefferson's private secretary, and William Clark, younger brother of Revolutionary War hero George Rogers Clark, left St. Louis in May, 1804, to explore the Louisiana Territory. Their expedition, a party of forty-five, traveled upstream on the Missouri River in three boats. They either rowed with oars or towed the boats from the shore with ropes. The group navigated the Missouri to its headwaters, crossed the Continental Divide, and continued on the Columbia River to the Pacific Ocean. The round trip of eight thousand miles took two years and four months.

Left: Cow trail, MT. Above: An old homestead, WY.

At mid-life, John certainly heard about the Gold Rush, when more than a quarter of a million people went to California by covered wagon, on horseback, or even on foot pushing wheelbarrows along the Oregon Trail. The Plains Indians, who had been fairly passive, felt threatened by this trail, which divided their hunting grounds. In 1856, rails crossed the Mississippi, connecting Rock Island, Illinois, and Davenport, Iowa. Mark Twain became a Mississippi River steamboat pilot in 1857, often passing under the bluff where John would be buried in 1901.

The Plains tribes began to resist the settlers' encroachment upon their hunting grounds, and in 1864, during the Civil War, Colonel John Chivington destroyed a Cheyenne village camped at Sand Creek in Colorado Territory. The first transcontinental railroad was completed in 1869. Special hunting trains were often organized, permitting hunters to shoot bison from the comfort of the cars. Indians found themselves unable to cope with the smoking iron horse as it continued to divide the land and deplete the bison.

When John was in his seventies, the prairie lands began to feel the commercial impact of the railroads. Texas longhorn cattle were driven by the thousands along the Chisholm Trail to the railhead in Abilene, Kansas. Several other Kansas towns had the dubious honor of being the cattle trail's terminus, but it was usually short-lived, since rail construction moved loading points west and south. Dodge City closed the trail-drive era and attained Boot Hill fame in the late seventies as the rails moved into Oklahoma and Texas.

To encourage railroad construction, the government granted alternate sections of land, up to ten miles on either side of the track, to railroad companies. While the Plains Indians were still fighting to preserve their hunting grounds, agents brought in settlers from all over the world to buy railroad land. Swedes, Norwegians, Poles, Czechs, Germans, immigrants of many nationalities and ethnic groups flocked to the prairies to make their homes. Russian Mennonite immigrants introduced Turkey Red winter wheat in 1874, two years before Custer's last battle in Montana.

The North American bison, usually called buffalo, numbered about sixty million at the time of Columbus. By 1870, the number was down to six million. By 1900, the animal was near extinction. Today there are about fifty thousand bison, some in government preserves and many privately owned.

Columbus Delano, U.S. secretary of the interior in 1873, wrote in his annual report, "I would not seriously regret the total disappearance of the buffalo from our western prairies, in its effect on the Indians, regarding it rather as a means of hastening their sense of dependence upon the products of the soil and their labors."

Left: Scotts Bluff National Monument, NE. Above: Bison (buffalo).

The 1880's and 1890's, John's last twenty years, witnessed dramatic changes in the heartland. The endless grasslands, which the Oregon-Trail emigrants had dreaded, were fenced into squares with barbed wire, and the meandering trails were replaced by straight, efficient dirt roads flanked by telephone poles and Osage-orange hedgerows. The adaptability of Turkey Red transformed the prairie into wheat fields and prosperous farms. Droughts, locusts, blizzards, and financial crises could not stop the thrifty, hard-working people who settled the prairies. The railroads made their produce marketable and also brought back goods to raise the standard of living.

By the time John died in 1901, cities and farms covered the tallgrass and mixed-grass prairies, ranches occupied the shortgrass country, and, in a bicycle shop in Dayton, Ohio, two young men were talking about flying. A breed of recklessly courageous people had overcome tremendous adversity to build a new country, and the new generation foresaw no limits to progress.

White-population pressure forced the "civilized" American Indian tribes of the southeastern United States into the Oklahoma Territory between 1824 and 1846. They were promised this land by the federal government for ". . . as long as the grass shall grow and rivers run." In the 1893 Sooner land rush all such rights were repudiated, and the Native Americans lost the land.

*Left: Railroad track, WY.
Above: Farmland, IA.*

Prairie Reverie

Flowering heads of Indian grass swayed hypnotically in a soft breeze. Bright yellow anthers hung precariously from their filaments. Would a gust of wind carry the pollen away, or would the pollen, dewy-wet at dawn, stick to the coat of a browsing deer; or would a pheasant, exploding from a cozy hiding place, leave a golden contrail?

Lying on my back, hidden and insulated from traffic by the tall grasses, I was serene. The world seemed safe and peaceful. Far above the grass, puffs of cloud scurried across a blue sky, and occasionally a flock of barn swallows swept over in pursuit of bugs. The gentle sounds of the prairie soothed my soul: the swish, swish of the tall bluestem, switch grass, and Indian grasses; the rustle of the leaves as a cottontail came near; and the shrill song of crickets and other little chirpers I wished I could name.

Time was a vapor beneath my grassy canopy and the floating cumulous woolies.

Suddenly in the distance appeared a column of dust and the glint of metal. Advancing from the southwest, the apparition came nearer. In what seemed only moments later, an army of men, some on horses, most of them marching, quietly passed by. The leader, arrayed in full Spanish armor, seemed proud and angry. His eyes, blazing contempt for the land that yielded no gold, were looking ahead for a place worthy of conquest.

As the disappointed army vanished, a lone rider approached from the east. The grass, bending before him, was as high as his saddle. Behind him I saw only open space with grass reeling and bowing in the wind. He rode by, settled in the saddle for a long ride. It was his eyes that caught my attention. Focused beyond the far horizon, they seemed not to see the prairie around them.

A red-tailed hawk soared overhead, and fleecy clouds became a covered-wagon train. Dust boiled up as wheels and hoofs beat into the earth. A cavalcade of wagons, carts, and even wheelbarrows moved doggedly across the land. Grass disappeared while oxen and horses grazed. These travelers, too, envisioned a goal far beyond the prairies, but their glance moved from side to side and back as if in fear. Picks, shovels, pans, and sieves hung from the wagon boxes.

Although grasses do not have showy blooms, the seeds are produced by inconspicuous flowers. The stamen, made up of the anther and filament, is the male, pollen-producing part of a flower. The pistil, the female reproductive structure, is composed of the stigma, the style, and the ovary.

Francisco Vasquez de Coronado, a Spanish explorer in quest of gold, led a 1541 expedition into what we now know as the Texas and Oklahoma panhandles and Kansas. He was searching for the Seven Cities of Cibola, which he believed to be filled with gold. From the time of Coronado until the Louisiana Purchase in 1803, little European activity occurred in the Great Plains north of Mexico.

*Left: Indian grass.
Above: Daisy fleabane.*

The long line of wagons came to an end, and the insouciant prairie grasses grew again to luxuriance.

A cloud momentarily blocked the sun, and it was early morning. A new wagon, without a top and pulled by heavy horses, stopped nearby. A man, a woman, and their children jumped out of the wagon and looked eagerly around. The man pushed a spade into the ground and smiled as he turned over the black prairie earth.

In the 1840's and the 1850's, thousands of settlers, gold-seekers, and Mormons used the Oregon and Mormon trails along the Platte River valley in their journeys to Utah and the Far West.

On a little knoll, the couple stood arm in arm for a few minutes. He put a stake in the ground, then with giant steps paced out a rectangle.

The prairies west of the Missouri River were considered only a corridor to the West until the 1860's and 1870's, when railroads made agricultural settlement feasible.

The children played in the imaginary house, running through doors only they could see. The woman looked a long time at the prairie, her face aglow but her eyes wistful. The man unloaded the wagon, beginning with the plow. Then they climbed into the wagon and headed back to the depot for another load.

Towering white clouds turned dark as they covered the sun. A pheasant answered a distant clap of thunder, and a cooling change of wind replaced the aroma of pitcher sage with the sweet smell of approaching rain. Present reality asserted itself as large raindrops knocked the pollen off the Indian grass overhead.

Left: Indian grass and pitcher sage. Above: Cumulous clouds.

The Plow

The six-shooter revolver is popularly regarded as the instrument that won the West. The truth is that the steel plow and the barbed-wire fence had far greater impact.

For two centuries, pioneer settlers on the eastern seaboard hacked and burned the forest to clear their farmland. When news arrived of a land to the west where there were no forests, common wisdom argued that lands not fertile enough for trees wouldn't grow corn either. Nevertheless, a few courageous souls set out for grass clearings in Ohio, Indiana, Illinois, and Wisconsin. They soon learned that these glaciated soils were a treasure trove.

The farmers used oxen and draft horses to pull cast-iron walking plows through the prairie sod. The strong roots scoured the cast-iron moldboard the first year, but the next season the heavy black soil, deprived of the massive root system, stuck to the plow and made it necessary to scrape the moldboard frequently. In 1837, John Deere, a blacksmith in Grand Detour, Illinois, built a polished-steel moldboard plow which resisted the sticky soil. Ten years later he was producing a thousand steel plows annually.

As settlers moved west into the prairies beyond the Mississippi, the plow, heavy as it was, became a fixture on the sides of the covered wagons. It would be needed to break the sod, plow fire guards, plow in hedgerow seedlings, and cut strips of sod for the family dwelling. A boy became a man when he could pull a straight furrow across a field.

Like ripping canvas, the grass roots gave way as twelve-inch strips of earth were turned over for the first time. The jangle of the harness, the snorting of horses, the sweep of the wind, and the occasional call of the meadowlark were the only other sounds as the plowman struggled with the reins and plow handles. Water in a stone crock, wrapped in a gunny sack, was his reward as the horses rested at the end of the furrow.

From Roman times to American Colonial days the plow, not much more than a stick with handles, was little improved. In 1797, Charles Newbold patented a cast-iron plow.

A walking plow basically consisted of a set of handles and a beam to which the plow bottom was attached. The plow bottom was made up of the cutting edge, called the share; a moldboard to turn the soil over; a landside riding against the furrow wall; and the framework, or "frog."

Riding plows were known as sulky plows. If more than one bottom was attached, they were called gang plows. Today, a tractor plow cutting six furrows is referred to as a six-bottom plow.

Left: Sunset near Niobrara River, NE. Above: Wheat and white eveningprimrose.

At best, breaking sod with a walking plow was slow work, so it wasn't until the large steam and gas traction engines were developed that the wholesale "turning over" of the prairie was accomplished. During World War I, it became every farmer's patriotic duty to plow as much land as possible in support of the war effort. Heavy iron tractors with names such as Oilpull, Mogul, J. I. Case, Twin-City, Avery, and many more arrived on the scene between 1910 and 1920. These huge engines inched their way across the plains at two miles an hour, relentlessly pulling twelve-bottom plows and turning grassland into America's breadbasket.

Plowing, whether with animal power or by tractor, required physical strength and endurance. Using the early tractors, plowing was a two-man operation, one man operating the tractor and another handling the plow levers. At the end of the field, as the tractor made the turn, the plowman walked along a narrow platform on the plow, pushing down the long handles to raise the moldboards. Then, almost immediately, he would drop the moldboards as the outfit headed back the other way. Sometimes both driver and plowman would take a short nap as the tractor wheels followed the furrow to the field's end a thirty-minute mile away.

In one generation the moldboard plow transformed the grasslands, millions of years old, into the most productive food factory in the world.

John Deere not only introduced the steel plow but moved farm-implement-making from the local blacksmith shop to the large-scale manufacturer with a dealer network. The company he founded has become the world's largest manufacturer of farm machinery.

Modern farmers often replace plows with chisel implements for conservation reasons. The practice is known as minimum tillage.

Left: Headed green wheat.
Above: Three-bottom plow.

The Dust Bowl

There were two kinds of dust storms in the 1930's. The big storms came in from a distance, maybe several hundred miles, advancing silently and ominously in a solid front of dark roiling clouds carrying millions of tons of topsoil. Dust from Oklahoma was red, and from Colorado and western Kansas either gray or brown. A more localized and relatively minor type of storm occurred on the eastern fringes of the Dust Bowl, arriving with the wind and picking up gray local dust from the fields beneath blue-white storm clouds.

I have vague but stirring memories of a beautiful spring morning in the early 1930's. The mulberry trees and our old hog barn and fences appeared in surreal golden hues, and I felt the pressure of the hushed atmosphere. The blackbirds were chattering in animated clusters. An electric force in the air was powerful enough to leave such impressions on a four-year-old.

Mom called for me to come in. It was not the ordinary call; her urgency made me run. She pulled me by the arm and slammed the door. Soon the room was dark except for the light from a kerosene lamp glowing on the kitchen table. The darkness seemed to be swallowing the light. Outside the window, the morning was black. The clock's ticking punctuated the silence.

The wind caught up with the dust and moaned through the cracks in the windows. Dust filtered into the room; someone coughed, and Mom clutched more tightly. I don't remember any conversation.

In the days before scientific weather forecasting, storms were a surprise. One summer day I saw surface dust whipping across the fields under white wind clouds. Mom was ironing with a kerosene iron when I ran inside to tell her dust was coming our way. We ran out to get the rest of the wash off the line, and by the time we were closing windows, dust was blowing into the house and doors were slamming.

The Dust Bowl was the product of a great ecological mistake. Overgrazed and exposed with the one-way plow, the shortgrass prairie region was vulnerable to the severe drought extending from 1933 to 1939 and became a windswept sea of dust.

Dust swept up into Montana and Wyoming on May 9, 1934, and moved eastward at 100 miles an hour, darkening East-Coast skies for two days. In March of 1935, twelve consecutive days of storms destroyed Nebraska's total wheat crop along with half of the Kansas crop and one fourth of Oklahoma's. Then on Black Sunday, April 14, the greatest black blizzard in history engulfed the whole region.

Seven times in the late winter of 1935, residents of Amarillo, Texas, experienced zero visibility due to dust, once for eleven hours. Throughout the region people lost their way, or their cars became stuck in drifts of dust. Even trains were derailed.

Left: Blowing dust.
Above: Red-winged blackbirds.

One day in the forties, I skipped high school classes to help Dad sow oats. It was a very cold day to be out on an open tractor. In the morning a bank of dark dust clouds moved in from the northwest, and soon I couldn't see the other tractor in the small field. I could barely see the drill-marker furrow in the dirt ahead of me. If the oats came up in straight rows that spring it was a wonder, because the visibility was so poor that the Farmall's radiator cap was only a phantom.

There was a difference in the two types of dust storms. The local storms usually picked up dust deposited by larger storms or, after a dry fall, scoured wheat fields without enough growth for cover; this damage could be minimized by chiseling the fields. Diverse crops, smaller fields, and realistic crop planning minimized the potential for harm.

Farther west in the shortgrass prairie country, the situation was different. Virtually whole counties in the panhandles of Texas and Oklahoma, in western Kansas, and in eastern Colorado and New Mexico were highly vulnerable to wind erosion. Part of the area was severely overgrazed between 1870 and 1930. The rest was plowed in the twenties and put to one crop, wheat. With the cultural practices of that time, even normal rainfall was barely enough to support the wheat crop.

In the 1930's the drought and the Depression were devastating to the country. Some say that both were caused by heinous exploitation of land and resources.

Over three million people were displaced by the crisis, ten thousand homes were abandoned, and millions of acres of farmland were left to grow weeds.

The drought of the 1930's should be viewed as a normal event of nature with a distinct possibility of recurrence.

Left: Windmill at sunrise.
Above: Blowing dust.

The Cottonwood Barn

A kind of shelter sadly belonging to the past, a barn is basic protection with no frills, warmer than a modern house even though snow filters through cracks in the cotton-wood siding. The warmth comes from a sense of well-being natural to a barn, where animals are safe behind doors closed against the cold.

In an old gray barn one winter evening, a half-dozen Shorthorns, heads poked through their stanchions, steamed as snow melted from their backs. A farmer and his son, heads pressed into cows' sides, milked into tin pails by the light of a coal-oil lantern hanging from a nail. Outside, snow was piled in drifts, shaped by a blizzard's turbu-lence around the barn. The hole which the boy had chopped in the stock tank's ice ten minutes earlier was already freezing over.

In the dark lean-to, cattle lounged on bright new straw hauled in by the farmer just before the storm, and at the north end of the barn sheep bleated now and then as ewes and lambs found each other. Sparrows, profiting from the animals' heat, nestled in crannies between the sheathing and the rough-hewn framework. A barn owl, perched above on the hay-carrier rope, watched. The mingled odors of dry alfalfa, hams curing in the oat bin, and confined animals; the flame's long shadows, and the lantern light reflected in hidden eyes; warm milk foaming in a bucket; and the good feeling about their livestock, warm and nearby, made the farmer and the boy feel richer than kings.

Even now, the barn's old timbers, its wood smoothed by animal bodies rubbing, its windows, and its ropes evoke memories and dreams, a magic peace no child of the television age can truly understand.

Barns have identifiable features that reflect regional, functional, and even ethnic characteristics. Black, creosoted barns are usually found in Kentucky; barns with adjustable side vents are tobacco-drying barns; and Amish barns, with their cantilevered overhangs, express a way of life.

Many Western prairie barns were constructed of available cottonwood lum-ber. As it aged, this wood became very hard and it warped, leaving many cracks in the barn. It is difficult to drive a nail into old barn siding or timbers made of cottonwood.

Usually called a sparrow, this most common of prairie birds is actually a finch, some authorities say. "House sparrow" is the proper iden-tification of this prolific bird, introduced into the United States in 1850 to combat cankerworms. Being vegetarians, house sparrows not only ignored the canker-worms, they became pests as they displaced more desirable species, such as bluebirds.

Left: XIT horse barn, TX. Above: Winter sunset, IA.

Search for the Ponderosa

Driving through the range land of Oklahoma, New Mexico, and Texas, Carol and I looked for sprawling ranch houses with quaint verandas, bunkhouses, corrals, and cowboys in the saddle. We traveled miles and miles of highways and country roads searching for something like the spacious "Ponderosa."

One evening, as we walked into a dingy Texas Panhandle cafe, business cards on the bulletin board caught our attention. The services offered were more contemporary than quaint: custom-built fences, cattle-hauling, grass-seeding, pond-digging, baling, horse-breaking, and much more. The twentieth century, we realized, had caught up with the rural Southwest.

The next day Carol pointed out a contractor building fences near Amarillo and called my attention to the huge cattle trucks on the road.

For the rest of the day we made a game out of transposing twentieth-century reality into nineteenth-century fantasy. A man in a pickup became a cowboy; a three-wheeler became a quarter horse. A glass-fronted high-rise became ranch headquarters, and a posh city residence was the ranch house.

As a former contractor, I could easily imagine a ranch-management officer in one of those glitzy banks calling a dozer man in Dalhart. "Say, Joe, I've got a map here of section twenty-seven showing a spot that looks wet and wooded. Could you get that cleared and drained so that we can get some production out there? And, say, bill us before the end of the year; we need the deduction."

The Shamburger Ranch, forty miles north of Dalhart, is a modern ranch. In the 1890's its range land was part of the largest ranch in the world, the XIT Ranch. Of its head-quarters near a natural spring, called Buffalo Springs, only decaying remnants of a wooden house, a stable with a blacksmith shop, and an adobe hut remain.

The spring is still there, a beautiful oasis in a sparse land. Turtles bask on fallen logs, and ducks spring up from the blue water. An eagle soars above the cottonwoods overhanging the little lagoon.

One section of land is one square mile, approximately equal to 169 average square city blocks. Fifty-seven sections would cover an area about one hundred blocks long and ninety-six blocks wide.

In 1879 the Texas state leg-islature set aside over three million acres of public land for the purpose of funding a new capitol. Three years later, this land was traded for the construction of the Texas state capitol. This land was the nucleus of what in 1885 became the XIT Ranch.

Left: Mesquite and prickly-pear cactus. Above: Nipple cactus; Texas horned lizard.

Nearby is a small, modern house occupied by ranch-hand Curtis Wyatt and his wife. Since the nearest town, Texline, is twenty-three miles away, they have a satellite dish and a radio tower.

The Buffalo Springs tract is now part of the Shamburger Ranch. Much smaller than the XIT Ranch, the Shamburger Ranch is large by most standards, containing fifty-seven sections. It is owned and operated by people who care about the land. The owner, from Dallas, flies in often, landing his plane on a grass strip next to the manager's house, to keep in touch.

Day-to-day operations center in the manager's house, a modest farm home. Nearby are a steel building, steel grain bins, and a scattering of tractors and farm implements.

The large bunkhouse with cowboys ready to hit the saddle is a thing of the past. Day workers are called from town when cattle need to be "worked"—branded, vaccinated, and castrated. The pickup truck has largely replaced the horse. Mr. Wyatt feeds winter supplemental "cake" to range cattle by driving into a pasture and turning on a siren. Cattle, accustomed to this, come running.

Open space, cattle, and hard-working people are the continuing reality of ranching. Perhaps the romance existed more in the minds of twentieth-century writers than nineteenth-century pioneers.

The original XIT Ranch covered three million acres, or 4,687 sections. Starting in the northwest corner of the Texas panhandle, the ranch, with a few jogs, extended more than two hundred miles southward along the New Mexico border. The average width was about twenty miles. Fifteen hundred miles of fence was built to divide the ranch efficiently.

Cowboys were paid bounty in winter months to kill wolves. Allen Stagg killed eighty-six wolves in 1896, sometimes by crawling into the dens after them. The last wolf in the area was killed in 1916.

Left: Prickly-pear cactus bloom. Above: Prickly-pear cactus plant.

The Wetlands

Walking through four thousand acres of what used to be the Inman wetlands, I see relicts of the once-marshy ground and surrounding prairie lands. Low pockets and winding hollows, not yet completely buried by the efficiency of modern agriculture, memorialize a land of potholes and meandering streams that a century ago were dry only in hot summer months. A few small patches of cattails remain where red-winged blackbirds hide their scarlet shoulders among the seed spikes. The tenacious cord grass grows in a small corner of a wheat field around a freshly dug drainage ditch. Like quarter notes on a stave, cowbirds perch on the fence of a native pasture.

Five acres of marsh remain undrained, rendering a primitive shadow on the farmland and accenting alkaline, gray soil not suitable for man's monocultures. Cottonwood and willow trees line the wet banks, and, from a hidden darkness in the undergrowth, a flicker's song floats serenely across the water. Mourning doves can barely be heard through the orchestra of grackles, dickcissels, meadowlarks, and frogs. I can only guess what lies beneath the stagnant surface: muskrats, water snakes, and snapping turtles, perhaps.

Lake Farland has become a wheat field, though some road maps still mark it. Dikes and deep ditches bound the fields to protect the land from flooding. Culverts feed into the ditches, draining water quickly to prevent standing water from ruining the crops.

My ancestors worked together to "improve" the wetlands, changing sauntering streams into unswerving ditches. Nature's intricate, irregular creation became a studied geometric design. My grandfather's generation, after hours of shrewd deliberating and self-indulgent arguing, determined to build the dikes and ditches. My generation leveled some of the land for irrigation.

Last November, I visited a relict marsh too small to attract any migrating waterfowl. My grandfather's contemporaries remember the geese and the ducks, thousands of waterfowl, stopping each spring and fall. In the early days of European settlement, Eastern hunters came west on the railroad to take advantage of the abundance of wild game. Several hunters' shacks once stood on higher ground overlooking the marshy

Wetlands are an important part of the prairie environment. In the north, lakes, rivers and potholes were formed by the ice-age glaciers. From Kansas south through Texas, rivers and shallow wetlands were formed by water and wind erosion.

Waterfowl and shore birds depend on wetlands and potholes for food, water, and rest as they migrate across the prairie states twice a year.

Left: Sunset, Hubbard Creek Lake, TX. Above: River bulrush.

areas. Old photographs document the harvest: ducks and geese hanging by their feet from an eight-foot pole borne by two men with shotguns.

My daughter may know about Inman wetlands only through written accounts, as I learned about the passenger pigeon. The last time our waterfowl brothers visited the Inman wetlands was 1977, five years before my daughter was born. That fall, a storm drenched the area with one of the largest floods of the past century; the birds followed instinctively.

When I lament the wetlands' demise, some neighbors point out that the flood that year was followed by a violent hail-and-sleet storm killing many of these migratory birds. While my neighbors justify the wetlands' disappearance with reference to nature's cruelty, I find it difficult to imagine what life would be like without the calls of Canada geese or the squawks of ring-necked, masked, and mottled ducks that still refresh themselves at Cheyenne Bottoms or Quivira.

I am told that an afternoon with a dozer would help nature start the flooding of the Inman wetlands again. If one culvert were to be filled with earth, the next rain would begin the process. In another century, my great-grandchildren might be able to see and hear the semiannual migration, and the Inman wetlands would again be a resting place along the central flyway in North America.

by Carol Schmidt

Only forty-six percent of the nation's wetlands remain. Losses in the prairie states are higher due to intense cultivation. The mallard duck population has declined thirty-five percent between 1955 and 1987. Northern pintails have lost sixty-five percent.

Deep, open reservoirs and large lakes do not supply the proper environment to sustain most waterfowl and shore birds. In Kansas only two significant wetlands remain, Cheyenne Bottoms and Quivira National Wildlife Refuge. Forty-five percent of North America's shore birds pass through them.

Left: Quivira National Wildlife Refuge, KS. Above: Canada geese, OH.

Observations of a Bulldozer Man

A bulldozer man has a very intimate connection with nature, something of a love-hate relationship. Even on a twenty-five-ton mass of hot steel, oil, and internal fire, he develops a keen sensitivity to the diversity of soil, rock, and root exposed by the blade. He senses the color, moisture, texture, smell, and purity of the earth, often falling in love with what he is violating.

I recall digging my first stock pond to provide water for range cattle. The fresh, earthy aroma was pleasant as the blade tore the deep, clinging bluestem roots and the earth. The soil's vulnerability was unmistakable, as the shallow black topsoil gave way to the gray of the sterile subsoil. Deeper yet, the mystery of ground water was revealed as little rivulets seeped from a sandy aquifer above a hardpan of clay.

Virgin tallgrass prairie soil often is fifty percent air space, ten percent humus, and forty percent solid earth materials. Tillage may reduce the volume of soil by half, squeezing out the air pockets. A square meter of tall bluestem sod may contain twenty-five miles of roots and hair-like rootlets.

Years ago, while I was digging into an embankment of a salt-water-disposal pit, a mother badger attacked my dozer with courage and ferocity in defense of her den. Undaunted by her massive opponent, she bit into the steel. Snapping turtles the size of basketballs and slimy muskrats tried to hide in the cord-grass perimeter, and redwings screamed from their cattail home as my tractor forced them into a wheat field nearby. Only twenty years old, this artificial brackish marsh already had a life of its own.

Snapping turtles often winter in muskrat lodges with underwater entrances. Oil-field salt-water disposal pits are illegal today.

The job of pushing down, piling, and burning Osage-orange hedgerows was common for my dozer. Before the use of safety cabs, this was a fairly dangerous task. Once, a thorny branch whipped across the tractor into my face, momentarily knocking me out. I regained my senses just before my dozer headed into a blazing burn pile. Cursing, wiping away blood, and clearing branches from the operator console, I reversed out of trouble, never stopping work.

Thorny Osage-orange hedge-rows were introduced to the mid-prairie states by settlers to fence in stock. After the introduction of barbed wire, Osage orange was used for fenceposts. Osage orange, often called bodark, is native to the South-Central states and was used by Indians to make bows.

The blood, sweat, and danger seemed part of the bond I shared with the natural world. Storms and ice twisted the trees, squirrels raided mourning-dove nests, mice and quail lived in fear of hawks. Yet spring brought new growth, the new song of the dove, and the crystal call of quail across the fields. The prairie land tests the mettle of its occupants, and, as a dozer man, I liked the challenge.

Left: Nine-spotted ladybug beetles. Above: Mourning doves.

For a time these furry, feathered, hard-shelled, and thorny homesteaders were mere diversions as I built ponds, terraces, and shopping-center parking lots. But as I became aware of their identities, their habits, and their resilience, I began to enjoy and appreciate them. I realized that they too had feelings, that the mother badger was crying for her young, that the redwings were angry, and that even the stoic turtles were shocked as I drove them out of their watery home. Still, it seemed almost sacrilegious to question my species' right of eminent domain, despite the prior claim of my new friends. The dozer rolled on for many years.

Little by little the years wore away the thrill of power and conquest. The dozer proved to be a fickle partner. It grew old, rusty, and worn before its time. The resilient prairie land spoke to me of values eternal, responsible, and beautiful. Steel, money, and business vied for my loyalty against sunset prairie bronzes and golds waving in the wind.

Last winter, on a very cold day, a little junco crashed against my window and lay there on the sidewalk, stunned. As I picked it up I could feel its heart beating. I took it inside to warm it by the fire. It revived and was frightened, so I took it outside and let it fly away, its black-and-white tuxedo a bit rumpled. I was happy that my little friend was feeling well again.

While man-made ponds and marshes and introduced hedgerows appear to be miniature ecosystems, they are not self-sustaining because of limited space and diversity.

Left: Muskrat, Cheyenne Bottoms, KS. Above: Prairie gentian.

To Have a Name

A mockingbird trilled through its repertoire, and I swear that the nearby cardinal had a Southern accent. Oklahoma's Lake Wister emerged from the night's tranquillity as the morning sun burned its misty covers away. On a high overlook on the lake's north side, I reveled in the morning's splendor.

From a rock road to the west came a roar of tires and the groan of a laboring engine. A large motor home pulled up to the lake's edge, and, before the dust settled, a family of four jumped out with cameras, ran to the guard rail, snapped a few photos, rushed back into their vehicle, and accelerated away. Time elapsed: thirty-nine seconds. The motor's irreverent noise had eclipsed a treetop duet's matins.

I recalled the Creation story in Genesis: "So out of the ground the Lord God formed every beast of the field and every bird of the air, and brought them to the man to see what he would call them; and whatever the man called every living creature, that was its name." Had the hasty family known the names of the nearby passionflower, the paw paw, the cardinal, and the mockingbird, perhaps they would have paid their respects.

Our children were in grade school when we discovered bird watching, "the name game." Before that time we knew little birds as sparrows and big birds as crows. V. Lee started the game by buying a bird book. One morning we packed the three little ones into the old Plymouth and took off west to the sandhills.

Marci had the sharpest eyes, spotting a flock of birds in some bushes. "Those are just sparrows," I said.

"Wait, Dad," Murray, old enough to read, hollered from the back seat. "Those aren't sparrows. Look at those white tail feathers when they fly. Those are slate-colored juncos."

We drove on. "Stop," Marci screamed. "Look over there in that tree, way up there."

Sure enough, there was a pretty red bird, calling "wish, wish, wish." I liked that one. So it went: Marci found them; Murray proudly named them; Beth, the little one, mimicked Marci; V. Lee smiled happily; and I drove, enjoying it, but a little embarrassed when other farmers passed us.

Bird watching is a very popular national pastime, and the prairie lands offer the greatest variety. This noncompetitive sport delights young and old, the beginner and the professional. Related activities, such as flower and butterfly identification, are popular also.

Bird guidebooks with color pictures, range maps, key identification features, and size and habitat information are essential. Keep a bird chart: a list of birds identified along with the date, time of day, and place. A calm, sunny morning is usually the best time to observe birds.

Left: Redheaded woodpecker. Above: Sphinx moth.

"The January One bird-watch" became a family tradition. We went out early in the snow armed with bird guides, binoculars, cameras, and Murray's bird charts. Over the years we learned to anticipate where certain birds would be, and we discovered that each species had its own habitat and style of flying. We had a standard route, not geographical but environmental. We included our yard, fence rows, hedges, pastures, lakes, and other areas, each with its own community of birds.

At first I could fool the kids with "superior eyesight." I would see a medium-sized bird on a power line a quarter-mile away and shout, "Sparrow hawk" (the local name for a kestrel). Driving closer, I was usually proved right. They soon caught on to my trick, which, of course, was knowing the sparrow hawk's habits. It didn't take long before we all identified flickers by their undulating flight patterns and chickadees simply because they were hanging upside down on dry sunflowers.

My family never reached the point where they could "do" a scene in thirty-nine seconds or even an hour, but the pleasure, peace, and love found will never be forgotten. To know the names of our prairie friends, the birds, animals, flowers, and grasses, made a difference.

Here are some details to watch for in identification: Nuthatches usually creep down tree trunks head first. Certain species, such as red-winged blackbirds, fly in large flocks, while orioles are solitary. A loud, harsh call often announces the kingfisher. Avocets wade in shallow water and have long, upcurved bills. Colorful male goldfinches change to a dull gray for the winter. Eagles and hawks usually soar alone, while vultures soar in groups. A scissor-tailed flycatcher has a very long, scissor-like tail.

Birds, the flying prairie flowers, offer a panorama of color, action, and sound as the seasons change.

Left: Painted lady butterfly. Above: American goldfinches, winter.

Silent Walk

I took a walk the other evening, making my way across a fallow field, rough, cloddy, with dry weeds knee-high, then along a boundary, winter wheat on one side and rustling milo stalks on the other. On the distant horizon the grain castles of Inman caught the last glow of the setting sun.

Fifty short years ago I used to tramp across these fields, imagining myself to be an explorer about to encounter wild wolves and buffalo; or, when the snow was deep and blowing, I was a Royal Canadian Mountie on a heroic mission. Most of my dreams came from reading *American Boy,* an adventure magazine filled with tantalizing stories of worlds to conquer with brawn and courage. I would take my Sears and Roebuck single shot and set out across the stubble fields ready for adventure.

No matter what the season, there were always birds and animals ready to gamble one bullet, staking life against my pride, not knowing that I would shoot only sparrows, crows, and rabbits. Even in a snowstorm I would run into a jack rabbit holed up in a snowdrift, and see snow buntings flying their hologram patterns, and hear geese high above.

I retraced my steps the other day, walking briskly, enjoying evening colors disappearing in the west; trying to recover memories. Coming across a charred stump, I realized how things had changed. The stump had been a mulberry tree in a fence row planted by birds sitting on a fence post. In the summer there was always a dickcissel singing in that tree, with badger diggings underneath.

The sun set early, this being a week from the winter solstice. I stood alone in the dark, a mile from the nearest road or farm, and I became aware that I was indeed more alone here than I used to be. I had not come across a single living animal or bird in the fields, not a jack rabbit, not a horned lark, not even the voice of a coyote. I listened, but only the wind in the milo stalks and a distant truck broke the silence. Gone also were the flights of geese and ducks.

Where crop cultivation is practical, wheat, corn, milo, and other cereals have replaced native prairie grasses and forbs in the prairie states, affecting the balance of birds, animals, and microfauna. In addition to the reduction of habitat, the use of agricultural fertilizers and chemicals is a factor in the changing balance of nature.

Fossil fuels, gasoline and diesel, are the foundation of the agricultural structure. Traction, fertilizers, herbicides, and insecticides are all derived from fossil fuels. No acceptable technology now exists to replace fossil fuels when supplies diminish.

Today, most decisions regarding the land are based upon short-term economic benefits (spanning a presidential term or, at most, one generation). Long-term consequences of current farm practices are largely unknown.

Left: Grain elevator silhouette. Above: Jack rabbit.

I recalled Rachel Carson's book, *Silent Spring*, remembering how angry I had been the first time I had read it. The book dealt with the inherent danger in the use of chemicals in industry and agriculture, and I had seen it as a threat to my commercial spraying business. I had been a pioneer in the spraying business and proud of it. I had killed trees under hundreds of miles of power lines for a utility company and had sprayed acres and acres of farm land to kill weeds and insects.

I had scoffed at Carson's alarmist views. She said chemicals were dangerous; I, with many other applicators, had known better. We were still alive.

In the 1950's most of the world recognized only tangible, immediate physical perils. Phrases such as parts per million, herbicide-resistant biotypes, and mutant chromosomes were out of our realm of understanding and interest. Dead weeds, aphids, and grasshoppers were wonders we expected and appreciated from technology.

Chemical cans had caution labels, but caution is a relative thing. When a spray nozzle clogged, I removed it from the holder, put it to my lips, and blew out the obstruction, and then exercised caution by wiping my mouth thoroughly. Spraying trees with 2,4,5-T in summer was hot, tedious work. To cool off and have some fun, we would spray each other mischievously with the solution. For caution's sake we took a bath every night.

In Vietnam, 2,4,5-T became Agent Orange.

Birds, like the miner's canary, portend environmental dangers. Since toxic residues and air pollution affect birds before people, a decline in bird population may serve as a warning of human peril. Long-term use of pesticides and herbicides is known to have produced resistant mutants, often more vigorous than the parent stock, thus worsening the original problem.

Left: Winter prairie.
Above. Plane spraying corn.

Prairie King

Practically speaking, what most of us are saying about the prairie ecology is rhetoric; our voices, so convincing to each other, seldom reach the ears of the movers and the shakers.

Farmers and ranchers own most of the prairie lands. They have the legal title, and they pay the taxes. They also have heroically accepted the responsibility to grow food for the world and to generate the economic base on which the prairie states rely.

Farmers have converted the native prairie grasses and wetlands to cultivation, while ranchers, as a rule, maintain the original prairie grasses for grazing.

Farms are feudal kingdoms; the natural flora and fauna are vassals with no rights. The kings of these domains have life-and-death powers much more sophisticated than the lords of medieval Bavarian castles ever dreamed of. The airborne arsenal at the farmer's disposal can kill millions of little creatures in moments. Larger animals, such as coyotes and water birds, were evicted long ago, when their space was appropriated for more production.

Yet the farmer is hardly a cold-hearted ecological villain. Production of food and fiber is something we all support every day. Most farmers and ranchers, aided by the federal Soil Conservation Service, protect soil and water as well as they can. History, however, shows that farmers respond to economic and social pressures just as other capitalists do. How farmers respond to ecological issues is only a reflection of what society has demanded of them.

Homestead acts parceled out land to pioneers with the stipulation that the land be plowed. Vast tracts of land were granted to early railroad companies, who in turn sold it to farmers for development. During World War I, official directives urged excessive plowing to support the war effort. As recently as ten years ago, federal funds were available to drain wetlands. From the 1950's on, land-grant colleges researched and encouraged the intensive use of fertilizers and potent chemicals for agriculture, always increasing productivity even while crop surpluses were a problem.

According to the federal Food Security Act of 1985, farmers must make a conservation plan by 1990 and implement this plan by 1995 if they wish to remain eligible for crop subsidies. The Soil Conservation Service offers technical assistance. Monetary aid is provided by the Agricultural Stabilization and Conservation Service.

The Food Security Act of 1985 is aimed primarily at excessive water runoff and unacceptable rates of soil erosion. The effects of fertilizer and other chemicals on ground water and soil are not addressed.

*Left: Wheat stubble, MT.
Above: Harvesting corn.*

Clearly, political and agricultural policies, once perhaps sound and well intentioned, need to be reviewed now.

Farmers, too, love a golden sunset and the song of a mockingbird. They respond to the delicate beauty of sea gulls hovering, almost within reach, over freshly tilled soil behind the plow. The farmer loves the land but also knows the joy of and need for production. Our world's demand for cheap food pressures farmers to put aesthetic and ecological concerns in the background.

The farmer is the lord of his kingdom, but like many bygone kings he lives in fear. The freedom to farm well, to practice good land stewardship, and to enjoy the process as a family effort has been lost to a more powerful emperor disguised as economic expediency. Low crop prices set by the economic gods clash with production costs, forcing farmers to extract more from the land to pay accounts due. The emperor wants his due now, even if it jeopardizes the future.

This scenario is oversimplified but real. The farmer is the conservator of the land, determining its natural ecological balance. Does the farmer have the freedom and motivation to preserve the productive and aesthetic qualities of the prairie land?

The complex linkage of foreign markets and competition, commodity markets, domestic politics, and weather remove control of farm-produce prices from the farmer. A cheap food supply, brought about by agricultural surpluses, creates a paradox. Individual farmers, in order to make a profit, meet low crop prices with more production, collectively increasing the surplus. Surpluses of perishables are wasteful.

Left: Planting wheat.
Above: Soybean field, IA.

The O'Hare Ecosystem

Only a few minutes ago, inside Chicago's O'Hare terminal, I had been one of thousands—passengers, family members, workers—all moving in different directions at different speeds. Now, waiting in the aircraft, there is plenty of time to watch the purposeful bustle, the parade of fuel trucks, food trucks, police cars, snowplows, and other planes. Little blue tractors pull baggage trailers; large tow tractors push and pull airplanes.

It occurs to me that O'Hare is a new ecosystem. It has grown and flourished here on prairie land, spreading under its own momentum. Human beings claim to manage it, but they are only parts of the whole. The shoeshine man, the ticket agent, the tractor driver, and all their mechanical and computer tools are components, like the wheels and numbers and hands of a clock. The O'Hare ecosystem is greater than the sum of its parts.

The lights blink; a flight attendant points out the exits. We are in motion, and the people and vehicles and buildings recede. This airport, this concrete-and-steel-and-silicon amalgamate, I reflect, is a mutant, the almost unrecognizable descendant of grasslands and swamps and animal instinct. Is it malignant or benign? All I know for certain is that it gets me to Wichita quickly; and I like that.

The plane rises; below us, all types of vehicles converge in streams of light to become Chicago. It is nearly dawn. Rich colors mingle over Lake Michigan, unexpectedly flash fire in skyscraper windows, and dissolve in sunlight.

We cross the urban boundary. The countryside, painted with snow and shadow, looks like a huge relief map. The austerity of square fields and straight roads is softened by nature's gentler touch: hills scattered across the plain, and creeks that twist and wind.

The airplane's wing flexes, cutting fiercely through unresisting wisps of cloud. Below, farmland gives way to city and factory, then reappears. Traffic mounts the succession of bridges that march down the Mississippi toward St. Louis and its proud arch. The region appears rich indeed, and part of me feels pride in two hundred years of American ingenuity and achievement.

O'Hare International Airport, the world's busiest air terminal, is built on the site of an old orchard. An average of 110 aircraft arrive or depart each hour. Every year almost sixty million people, 160 thousand per day, arrive at or depart from O'Hare. More than forty thousand people are employed there. The longest runway extends thirteen thousand feet, or two-and-a-half miles.

O'Hare International occupies seven thousand acres, almost eleven square miles. By comparison, an average Midwestern grain farm covers a thousand acres. The old XIT ranch in Texas covered three million acres. It was 428 times the size of O'Hare.

Left: Ajuga. Above: Arkansas River, Wichita, KS.

Birds migrate annually; airplanes migrate daily. I wonder how much more we can accelerate nature's tempo without fatally sacrificing quality of life. Below, in rural Missouri, there is still woodland sheltering wild turkeys, squirrels, and bobcats. There are dogwoods waiting to bloom.

Our plane's shadow grows larger. It looks as if the little blue baggage tractor beat me to Wichita. Here is another new prairie ecosystem, somewhat smaller than that at Chicago. Is this ecosystem as fragile as the one it has displaced? Are its denizens endangered species, like the bobcats and the dogwoods?

I am nearly home now, driving slowly through the sand hills north of Burrton. A cluster of pheasant cocks shows up in brilliant reds, blacks, and browns against the snow. I stop and open the door, and they flee. A chickadee hangs upside down from a withered sunflower. The bitter cold is softened a bit by the bronze and amber of little bluestem and Indian grass, plus a few old catalpas and a strong sun. A red-shafted woodpecker blazons the scarlet secret under its wings as it glides onto a dead cottonwood.

I pick up a handful of sandy earth and walk through the sparse, lisping grass to the top of a hill. The wind cuts viciously through my jacket, and I run back to the car. It feels good to know that nature is stronger than I am.

An ecosystem is a community of organisms, in nature flora and fauna co-existing in an environment. Ecosystems often become self-sustaining units over a long period. A large ecosystem may be a complex of smaller ecosystems. Potholes in Minnesota are small ecosystems that are also part of the larger prairie ecosystem. A river valley is a discrete unit, but it is still part of a whole. A farmstead may harbor its particular population of birds and small animals, yet it remains part of the new agri-prairie ecosystem. What the removal of one organism in a small system can do to the health of the whole is often hard to measure.

Left: Little bluestem.
Above: Sunflowers.

Metamorphosis

The television newscaster was very analytical, discussing the alleged improper conduct of a senator. On another network was a commercial for an upcoming "movie of the week," with screeching cars careering through littered streets while unsavory characters stood watching on the corners. On yet a third channel an old man superabounded in violent indignation over passages in a recent book.

V. Lee brought a green twig into the room with a chrysalis attached upright, supported by silken threads. The miracle of life replaced the threshold of mayhem in our house.

A few days later a beautiful swallowtail butterfly emerged; its wings were delicate, translucent. As the life forces flowed through its body the wings took on form, color, and strength. Very carefully, we took it outside, and we were soon rewarded by the sight of this beautiful creature airborne in its element.

The world of the swallowtail is free, available to us all. To find this joy, we need to break the silken cords of our own chrysalis. At dawn we can inhale the fresh air and watch as dewdrops form on the grass. We can hear the night sounds of owls and coyotes give way to a chorus of birds and crickets, and feel the chill of dawn come as a late frost slowly creeps across the prairie. We may wait for the moment when the direct rays of the sun break over the horizon, setting ice crystals afire.

We can let go of that macho facade, take a deep breath, get down on our knees and touch a wild rose. We can see the dew on the petals and smell the fragrance. Better yet, let's show a little child these treasures and enjoy the process with abandon.

Let's forget the high heels. We'll let the wind blow our hair, climb over a barbed-wire fence, step over cow chips, and run to the top of a hill to see the mist in a valley. Let's tell the children about the romance of the prairie chickens booming in the distance.

We shall find that each sunrise is different and that some are particularly special. Every year, during the equinox, the sun crosses the equator on the first day of spring and again on the first day of fall. On these days the sunrise or sunset is always exactly east or west of wherever you are.

Over six hundred species of butterflies play an important role in our country's ecology as plant pollinators. Butterflies are very dependent on specific plants and habitats. An egg laid by a butterfly is the first stage of life; later the eggs hatch into caterpillars, which are voracious. Since a caterpillar skin cannot expand, the growing caterpillar sheds its skin several times. During the last molt it attaches itself to a plant and forms a chrysalis, a protective covering, in which the butterfly forms.

Authorities use differing terminology to describe the butterfly life cycle. The caterpillar may be called the larva, the chrysalis may be known as the pupa, and the shedding of caterpillar skin is also called molting. The transformation from caterpillar to butterfly is known as metamorphosis.

Left: Sunrise, Flint Hills, KS. Above: Roughseed clammyweed.

We'll pick an east-west road and watch the sun go down in the middle of the road. Ten minutes before sundown we'll say, "It's impossible. The sun is way too far south." But as we watch, we shall see its curved trajectory glide into the center of the road. (Be very careful to not look directly at the sun).

To say that I enjoyed a sunset, or that I saw a pretty flower, or that I snapped a gorgeous picture of a Wyoming landscape is not good enough. The pleasure and the value found in the natural world come from close contact with flora and fauna . . . identifying, studying, and observing life cycles.

To see a great white bird splash down into a lake is a breathtaking sight. To know that it is a white pelican, to realize that it has a wing span of over nine feet and that it is migrating from the Gulf Coast to Canada, greatly enhances one's interest. Then to watch the birds swim in groups, to see them "herd" schools of fish, surround them, and in unison tip over and scoop the fish into their large pouches is spectacular.

The beauty of nature is subtle. It does not clamor for your attention, but it is always there to be your friend. It is as near as the robin singing outside your window.

The yucca giant skipper caterpillars feed on the leaves of the yucca plant, then bore into the plant's crown, overwinter there, and emerge in the spring to become large butterflies. The same plant is host to the yucca moth, which picks up pollen in one plant and flies to the flower of another. It lays its eggs in the ovary, at the same time depositing the pollen in the stigma. The reproduction of the moth and the yucca plant depend on this symbiotic relationship.

Left: Common milkweed. Above: Equinox sunrise; yucca (soapweed).

Your Own Prairie

The pristine prairie was an ever-changing panorama of color and texture. Tender, green shoots bursting through last fall's brown foliage became bluestem and Indian grass almost as tall as a man on a horse. A profusion of flowers changed the scene weekly . . . prairie violets and blooming chickasaw plums were followed by blue-wild indigo, catclaw sensitivebriar, and prairie gaillardia. In midsummer, coreopsis, butterfly milkweed, and coneflowers reigned, soon to be deposed by the taller blazing star, compass plants, sunflowers, and goldenrods.

Everyone longs to connect with the earth and its natural issue. Perhaps we have buried memories of ancestral campfires and the days of hunting mammoth and bison *antiquus* in tall grasses. A walk in a prairie stirs these ancient intuitions.

Intimacy with the prairie is a therapeutic pleasure that eludes many modern Americans. Time, surroundings, vocation, money, peer pressure, and other barriers make daily communion with the natural world seem difficult. But it needn't be. A little corner in a back yard or garden, maybe only a square yard, planted to a few prairie grasses and a prairie flower or two would be a start. The thrill of watching a compass plant bloom, the aroma of a pitcher sage, and the rustle of bronzed little bluestem makes it well worth the effort.

Prairie restoration on a community level or naturalization of a park are exciting ways to get in touch with nature. Tracts of any size can be transformed inexpensively into living exhibits of the land as it was. The University of Wisconsin Arboretum in Madison contains an example of a beautiful public prairie large enough to offer the experience of walking through the tall grasses. Deere and Company has a prairie plot near the John Deere Museum in Grand Detour, Illinois, illustrating the variety of prairie plants. The concept of natural, indigenous landscaping for parks, schools, corporate centers, farms, and suburban dwellings is growing.

A striking example of using natural resources to landscape is the farmstead of Don and Pat Adelman near Madison, Nebraska. Their place was a cornfield in 1981, but now it has the look of a mature farmstead since they moved in native trees and shrubs from nearby pastures and wastelands. The Adelmans used a hydraulic tree spade to move about four hundred trees, some nearly thirty feet tall. The trees blend beautifully with

A general description of the "pristine" prairie can never be comprehensive due to climatic, geographic, and historical differences. Generally grasses and forbs were predominant, but their species and physical characteristics varied greatly. A prairie might have been sparse shortgrasses interspersed with sagebrush, or mile after mile of mixed-grasses, or tallgrasses surrounding potholes with bulrushes and sedges.

There are accepted precedents in nature that support theories of inherited or collective memory. Upland sandpipers "remember" to fly from Argentina to their North American breeding grounds generation after generation to rear their young. Many monarch butterflies migrate from their wintering place, the Sierra Madre in central Mexico, through the prairies into Canada, where they lay their eggs and die. The new generation, which has never been to Mexico, concludes the migration by flying back to the Sierra Madre the following fall.

*Left: Pitcher sage.
Above: Browneyed-susan.*

the countryside and the wildlife. Mr. Adelman comments that each tree has its own personality and says it's a shame that most farms aren't landscaped.

Suburban tracts, wastelands, irrigation tailwater pits, and other spots where you simply want to enjoy something unique are perfect places to try no-mow landscaping.

Patience is the key to prairie projects. Some of the grass and forb seeds do not germinate the first year. A prairie evolves; the first year weeds are guaranteed, the next year perennial forbs (prairie flowers) may bloom and some grass may show, and the third year you can expect to see your basic prairie.

A small acreage, of course, cannot become a true, ecologically balanced prairie, because the larger animals cannot exist there. Nevertheless, you will be surprised at the variety of butterflies, tiny creatures, and plants that will come to join you.

Researching to find a list of original species of grasses, flowers, shrubs, and trees is a rewarding experience in itself. County extension agents, state land-grant colleges, wildlife agencies, and seed companies can usually supply information.

Restoring aspects of the prairie ecology offers many exciting opportunities. It can be as simple as leaving a dead tree for woodpeckers to nest in; allowing roadside ditches and fence rows to develop into natural habitats instead of mowing and clean cultivation; or providing unmowed corners in manicured lawns, golf courses, and parks. Often, if given time, natural prairie seeds dormant for many years will germinate and grow in undisturbed areas.

Left: Catclaw sensitivebriar.
Above: Mixed prairie grasses.

The Land Speaks

Outside, walking against the Montana winter sleet, the Burrtons were in their element, joking and jostling, but the mood changed as they stepped into the Third National Bank's conference room. On a glossy table were the Burrtons' financial statements, neatly stacked, exposed to the world. Walking naked outside would not have been more chilling to the family. The ranchers—grandfather John, son Roger and his wife Molly, and grandson John, Jr.—were there to discuss strategies to avert bankruptcy.

Across the table were the bank comptroller and the men from the Farm Credit Services. At the head of the table sat a very annoyed banker, and at the other end was the source of his annoyance, an old Sioux named Luther Tall Bear. Great-great-grandfather Jerome Burrton's will had specified that in such matters the land itself should forever have a voice . . . in the person of the oldest American Indian in the county. No one had ever taken this strange clause very seriously.

The comptroller, the bank's spokesman, talked in a matter-of-fact monotone as he handed out flow charts. He concluded, with a nod toward the Burrtons, "Your ranch has been impacted by the distressed agricultural economy, generating a negative internal rate of return and jeopardizing the position of the creditors. It is obvious," he added with an air of discovery, "that the annualized bottom line must be upgraded. In real terms at the ranch, this means more animal units per acre, plowing more land for cash crops, and above all cutting expenses. . . . I repeat, cutting expenses.

"Do we all understand?"

All eyes turned toward the Burrtons. Roger, embarrassed and angry, exclaimed, "I just don't . . . , really, we can't. The large tractor's shot. We're overgrazing the range right now. I just don't see how you can expect. . . ."

"Now just a minute," the comptroller interrupted. "Don't take this personal, Roger. It's not us telling you what to do, it's the bottom line on this spread sheet that's telling you. I'm sorry, but that's it."

The shortgrass prairie, just east of the Rocky Mountains, extends from Texas to Montana. Extremes of weather— hot summers, very cold winters, high winds, and drought—are features of the northwestern plains. Rainfall here averages ten to twelve inches annually.

Large cattle and sheep ranches are found here. Up to thirty acres of grassland are required to support one cow. Where terrain and moisture permit, farms are found among the ranches. Many ranches operate dryland or irrigated farm operations to stabilize feed supplies and provide cash flow.

Dominant grasses are blue grama and buffalo, growing to a height of five to ten inches. An unusual feature of buffalo grass is its reproduction through stolons, above-ground spreaders, which take root every two to four inches. Buffalo grass also produces seed.

Left: Missouri Breaks, MT. Above: Purple coneflower.

Silence. A chair squeaked at the far end of the table. The old Indian stood slowly and cleared his throat. The bank president propped his head in his hands and rolled his eyes. Luther Tall Bear spoke. "I was asked to come talk for the land; now I hear a piece of paper speaks for the land." He paused, then said, "Who was asked by the hills and rivers to speak? When did the east and the west or the north and the south say, 'Speak for me'?"

Half amused, everyone listened as he went on. "The land has been speaking since the dawn was born. In a time long before our grandfathers, the wind in the waving grasses and the thunder of the sky were the word. Our voices are only a ripple in a brook, and your paper is less than a dry leaf in a whirlwind."

"Now see here," the banker stormed, but the old Indian waved him off and continued.

"If you walk slowly into a prairie alone in the spring, you can hear the bees swarming and woodpeckers tapping; lie on your back, feel the cool earth, see and hear the geese in the sky, smell the wild rose, and taste a blade of grass. You will know that this is good, and your heart will listen to the land and know what is right."

Luther Tall Bear turned to go, looked back and added, "If we do not listen now, the land will speak to us in whirlwinds of dust for a long time and then, when we are gone, grass will grow again." He walked out of the room straight and tall.

Eighteenth-century European settlement forced the Sioux people from their forest homes in Wisconsin and Minnesota to the northern prairies. Horses were new to the Sioux culture as they developed a nomadic, bison-hunting lifestyle in the 1800's. The Sioux were forced onto reservations after U. S. troops massacred the Indians at Wounded Knee, South Dakota, in 1890.

Left: Prairie rose.
Above: Prairie stream.

Introduction: Profiles

We had a wonderful time meeting and talking with the people featured in the profiles that follow. Most of the interviews were serendipitous, all were spontaneous and unrehearsed. Wherever we explained our goal of producing a book about the prairie land, we struck a chord.

Whether young or old or in between, everyone we visited was full of life and purpose. They were friendly people, concerned about their fellow citizens and about the earth, independent, typically proud of their homes and their work. Even those who were facing personal or financial setbacks seemed to draw courage from their love of the land.

Harold Bals of rural Loup City, Nebraska, exemplified this love of the land and the enthusiastic self-reliance we often found. Harold told us how as a young man he had enjoyed working in the grassland hay fields near Broken Bow. "I fell in love with the grassland," he said, "and I decided, by God, that's what I wanted to do."

He lives with his wife on a modest, charming farmstead, a dog at his side, chickens clucking and scratching, and sheep bleating as they wander across the yard. Their 540-acre ranch, once cultivated, now is covered with regenerated bluestem, side oats grama, and blue grama grasses.

Among those interviewed, opinions about the state of the environment varied. A few people had probably never thought about the future ecology beyond a few years or a generation at most, while others were deeply concerned about the future. The question of whether man's relationship to nature is as master or brother evoked differing reactions. All interviewed agreed: we must take care of the land.

Everyone had some close connection with the land. Sometimes we felt that it was this intimacy that generated the courageous, vibrant spirit we witnessed. It was a refreshing and encouraging experience to visit our prairie neighbors from Texas to Minnesota, and from Ohio to Colorado.

Mil Penner

Carl Schmidt

Left: Harold Bals, NE.

"Aha! We Will Plant a Prairie"

Botanist Nina Leopold Bradley and her husband, Charles, manage the Leopold Nature Reserve near Baraboo, Wisconsin. She has studied wildlife extensively in the United States and Africa. As a child in the 1930's, she helped her father, Aldo Leopold, restore native prairie grasses and flowers on a worn-out farm. Chirping rose-breasted grosbeaks, nuthatches, and goldfinches accompanied our conversation with Nina Bradley.

". . . Then we decided, 'Aha! We will plant it to prairie,' which we did. We planted the prairie seeds, and in five years, we had a really good-looking prairie.

"Every week from the first of June until the first of November, the colors and the texture of the prairie change. We start out with the delicate little early spring flowers, like the lupine and blue-eyed grass, and the very soft grasses. The silphiums [compass plants] and the prairie dock are now six and seven feet tall, bundles of yellow flowers. The purple liatris is just beginning to bloom. The little gerardia, the little soft purple flowers, are blooming. The yellow coneflowers are in bloom, and purple coneflower. Next week, it'll be different. Each week, the prairie changes, and it is much more exciting than a flower garden. In the fall, the colors of the grasses are so exciting, as you well know.

"Among the grasses planted, I think my favorite is prairie drop seed; and side oats grama, big blue, little blue, Indian, switch, and dune grass. . . .

"When Dad bought the property, it had been misused. In 1935, it was one big cornfield, just stubs left. Of course it produced very poor corn. You could see five miles down Levee Road; there was nothing. He had been involved at the University Arboretum, restoring an old farm to its native vegetation. . . . What did it look like before white men took it away from the Indians? That was Dad's motive, so he started out by planting prairie and planting pines and planting hardwoods by acorn, if you please. He didn't even have the little trees; he planted acorns; and I can show you the trees that he planted. . . .

"In 1968, the area was put into a natural area, the Aldo Leopold Memorial Reserve, in which six landowners put their back forties under common management. This was an experiment in private ownership of land for a purpose. This is all marginal land; it is not good agricultural land. The idea was how best to use it.

"I would say the principle [of the land ethic] is to treat land with love and respect, and to assume that we as individuals are a part of the landscape; that we are a part of the whole system, and that we should act accordingly, and not assume that it is all there just for our desires. But I think the most important thing that Dad said is that land should be respected and loved. You can't respect and love land unless you have some feeling for the land. That's why I think it is so important to be a farmer or to have a garden or to have a school forest or to do something with the land.

Aldo Leopold reshaped the conservation philosophy of America. A few paragraphs in his book, A Sand County Almanac, *shifted conservation viewpoints from a people-centered perspective to an ecological-community perspective. Leopold perceived a land ethic going beyond the necessity of conservation for human survival, in which people live with the flora and fauna as joint tenants on earth.*

Leopold developed his philosophy experientially. He graduated from Yale University's school of forestry, served as a forester in the mountains of New Mexico and Arizona, created a department of game management at the University of Wisconsin, and rebuilt the land on a ruined farm along the Wisconsin River. Leopold helped organize the Wilderness Society in 1935 and worked to establish the Wisconsin University Arboretum. He died fighting a grass fire in 1948, before A Sand County Almanac *was published.*

Left: Nina Leopold Bradley, WI. Above: Aldo Leopold Shack, WI.

"There's one place in [*A Sand County Almanac* where] Dad said, 'Until the land ethic becomes a part of philosophy and a part of religion, it can never work.' You'll find it in there. To me, the love of the land was Dad's religion. It had nothing to do with the ceremonies of the church. To me he was the most religious man I've ever known. . . .

"[I remember] visiting my father's mother in Iowa. Mother was bundling us all up, getting ready to go to church, and my grandmother, Dad's mother, waved good-bye to us, and said, 'I'm going to my church.' She went out on the bluff of the river, where she had her bench, and that was her church.

"I would think that what Dad did here is an example of second-home development that we might try to sell to people today. If you want an experience in handling the land, how about buying an acre that's ruined and see what you can do. Even a city block. Dig up the concrete, start with a little square meter, and plant something that belongs there.

"I'm more pessimistic [about the environment] by the day. I really feel more depressed as I read this week that the maple trees are dying in New England of acid rain. I think, my God, can you believe it? It isn't just the maple trees, it's the whole ecosystem. . . .

"I think we've got to start discriminating between our needs and our wants. We've got to start reducing our demands on the earth. Don't we?"

Mixtures of prairie grass and prairie wildflowers can be planted on tracts ranging in size from a square meter to several acres or more. Seed sources should be in an area similar to and as close to the planting site as possible. Since prairie plants germinate slowly, fertilizer will serve only to give weeds a head start.

Provide a firm seed bed with only enough loose dirt to cover most of the seeds, and plant the grasses and the perennial flowers simultaneously. Do not be disappointed if good results are not visible the first year; some seeds may sprout the second year. Mow the weeds about six inches high several times the first year. Do not use chemical weed control; it will kill the flowers. Keep in mind that these are prairie plants, so water only in a manner to which they are naturally adapted.

Left: Painted lady butterfly. Above: Wisconsin River, WI.

"The Delicate Balance"

Former Governor Arthur A. Link has had a long and active political career in North Dakota. He was a state representative from 1947 to 1970, a Member of the U. S. House of Representatives from 1971 to 1972, and North Dakota's governor from 1973 to 1981. More recently he served as chairman of the North Dakota Chapter of the Nature Conservancy and chairman of the Centennial Commission of North Dakota.

"I'm a first-generation offspring of parents who homesteaded the home farm in the year 1907, so my memory goes back to the 1920's as a child growing up in a very rural setting where a great deal of the land was native prairie.

"The settlers that came in and claimed their homestead rights were required to break up, to plow a certain percentage of the claim and cultivate it.... But before any of this took place, of course, it was all prairie. Practically all of the land was covered with grass, and grass of good quality. There's a grass they call the buffalo grass. That's one of the better grasses, a short, pretty grass.... The prairie's full of flowers; the primrose—some call them gumbo lilies. The very earliest was the spring crocus [pasque flower]. Then we have the bluebells, the sweet peas, the little violets....

"After [my wife and I] were married, I'd come home from the fields.... I'd stop along the way and pick a bouquet of sweet peas or crocuses and bring them home. And the wild rose, of course, the wild prairie rose.

"I think those of us who were born and raised in what is called the West River Country—that area south and west of the Missouri River—are partial to our home territory.... We see certain beauty in the eastern part of the state; we think the flat land and the rich agricultural area of the Red River Valley has a fascination all its own. But I guess we've lived so close to nature all our lives, we see that the impact of civilization on the [Red River Valley] country doesn't leave much in a natural state. Up in our country, there's so much that's still native.

"As a Christian believing that God created this universe and provided all of these things, I think we look at the delicate balance that's embodied in native circumstances, and we must take a lesson from that. Whenever man does anything to upset that balance, it changes things that can ultimately affect our survival.

"I gave a talk last January, and I gave a personal rundown of how the creek that I grew up on has changed in my years. When I was a kid growing up, it was a deep creek with fresh water in it that flowed most of the summer. Now it doesn't anymore; it's filled with silt and sediment. It's dry now; there isn't any water in it. I termed my speech 'The Death of a Creek'....

In 1982, the Nature Conservancy, a nonprofit organization dedicated to preserving the nation's natural heritage, purchased the Cross Ranch, north of Bismarck, North Dakota. Originally the Gaines Ranch, it was renamed the Cross Ranch after the Maltese Cross brand once used by Teddy Roosevelt on his ranch in the western part of the state. Part of the land, with its significant natural and archaeological history, is being retained as a nature preserve. Roaming the preserve are forty head of bison that make up the Centennial Buffalo Herd, one of Governor Link's centennial projects. The North Dakota Parks and Recreation Department manages 260 acres as the Missouri River Primitive State Park. South of the Cross Ranch, two-hundred-year-old cottonwood trees stand near the banks of the Missouri River in the Smith Grove Wildlife Refuge.

Left: Arthur A. Link, ND.
Above: Capitol, Bismarck, ND.

"This whole thing gets down to a matter of philosophy and ownership of land. We have developed a philosophy that ownership of anything [means it's] yours to do with as you wish.... But from a natural standpoint and from a natural heritage ... we're merely tenants on this land. There are generations unborn that must also have a place to live and must also depend on the good earth to produce the food and fiber. If one or two or three generations dissipate that valuable resource, what will history record us as? Mere rapists of the land? Our society and our husbandry are driven by the same engine that drives our whole economy—the dollar sign. It's all a matter of making a profit.... There's no long-term concern. Not really.

"The present federal program is putting greater demands on farm operators. I think a nation that enjoys the abundance of low-priced, in fact, cheap food that we do, has to take stock of where that cheap food is coming from.... The American farmer is one of the most efficient workers in the world in terms of ability to produce in abundance and at a low price. So whatever tax money the public puts into the government subsidy program they're getting back by an abundance of cheap food. It costs the American workers about fifteen percent of their disposable income to buy food.... I think in many countries it costs fifty percent....

"Man's survival depends upon [the natural environment].... Man cannot survive alone ...; so they go hand in hand. I think that there are some terribly frightening things happening in the world in terms of the destruction of the rain forests and the speed with which we're eliminating them, and all of the natural wildlife.... The concern for the environment [should be] paramount; it's just absolutely essential."

West of Bismarck along Highway 10, a plaque near New Salem marks the meeting of an American Indian with one of the early settlers plowing his land. On the plaque is the story of the Native American, who, after observing the plowing operation for a short time, remarked pointedly, "Wrong side up."

The West River Country of North Dakota, the area south and west of the Missouri River, contains Theodore Roosevelt National Park, commemorating the twenty-sixth President's conservation efforts. An avid outdoorsman, Roosevelt set aside more acres to the national forests than any President before or since. He described the Little Missouri River Badlands as a "land of vast silent spaces."

Left: North Dakota sunset. Above: Smith Grove State Wildlife Refuge, ND.

"The Sod House Is a Symbol"

Stan and Virginia McCone and their five children reside on a small farm in the sparsely settled farm country of southwestern Minnesota, near Sanborn. In 1987 Stan built a sod house near their farm home to strict pioneer specifications. He resigned his position as a cattle buyer for a large packing company in 1988 to set up his own business.

Stan: Well, a lot of people have asked me, why did you build this sod house? The pioneers that came out here to settle these prairies. Why did they do it? Why did they leave a farm in Wisconsin with fences and water, or a home in Pennsylvania where they had wood and canned fruit in the cellar and a brother down the road? Why did they come out here onto this prairie. . . ? They wanted to be free. . . . I worked for a corporation for twenty-three years, and they more or less told me when to get up and when to go to bed and what to do and what not to do. I wanted to be free. The sod house is a symbol of people basically wanting to be free.

Virginia: One historian that I read put [sod house numbers] at hundreds of thousands in a five-state area, probably the northern plains states, which would have been the Dakotas, Minnesota, Kansas, and Nebraska. Sod houses were built here in about the 1870's.

Stan: When the settlers came onto these prairies, all they had was grass. There weren't any trees. Well, you either had lumber from a railroad brought in to build some kind of house, or you just went out with your breakin' plow for sod. . . . Plowing it sounded like the ripping of a giant canvas, and they ripped that loose into furrows. They took this sod, cut it probably four to six inches thick, and then sectioned it usually into two-foot-long blocks. Then they turned the grass side down, and, just like blocks, built that into walls. Then they either bought some lumber from the closest place they could and did a roof and put sod up on it; or maybe they even could find some cottonwood poles or cedar poles, off in ravines or cricks somewhere, and they used them to make a roof. In a sod house built right, it's very cool in the summer and warm in the winter.

The house dimensions are twenty-one by thirty-six, that's outside. I think there's between three and four acres of sod in it. We estimated 300 thousand pounds of sod in here. [The walls] are probably seven feet tall. They've settled about eight or nine inches. Fortunately, we went high enough before we quit. . . .

I've seen pictures of sod houses in the 1800's with regular rafters, just like we built with two-by-fours, and regular board sheathing and regular tar paper.

A lady that homesteaded with her husband south of Laverne in the 1870's wrote her family and said, "It's beautiful, beautiful country. The flowers are magnificent. There's all colors of little flowers out there, and bunches and clumps of them. It's beautiful."

Prairie-sod building blocks were made out of plowed strips of earth and matted grass roots cut into two-foot lengths. Adobe bricks, on the other hand, were made of wet earth mixed with grass or straw, then molded and dried in the sun. It appears that sod construction was popular in the tallgrass regions, while adobe was preferred in the shortgrass areas.

Sod-house blocks, usually twelve inches wide (depending on the plow), were laid side by side with every third block being laid crosswise to tie the two rows of blocks together. The walls were two feet thick. Many sod houses had wooden floors, wood-framed windows and doors, and several rooms. There were also very temporary dugouts in ravines with one side sodded up.

Left: Stan and Virginia McCone, MN.
Above: Chicory.

I think the native prairie had flowers that God naturally gave that prairie to bloom at different times, at different seasons. This sod house, when we built it, we got done in the fall, we had all kinds of little blue flowers, delicate little flowers growing out of the sides of the walls.

Virginia: You read about the prairie woman going out in the spring throwing the flower seed that she'd saved up there on the roof. In a wet year they'd bloom. The woman bore a lot of the burden, and she's kind of the unsung hero behind it. Life was tough.

Stan: It's quite a feeling . . . , plowing sod that has never had a plow in it, and the little flowers are down there, and you're plowing them up. It gives you a little feeling of trespassing. It just rips and cracks and pops, and it comes out in ribbons. [An old homesteader told me years ago], "I seen 'em plow fifty feet of sod with a walking plow, cut it with a knife, put a chain on it, and pull the whole strip with a team of horses." That root system is so intense that it just holds together like a carpet.

Thoreau said, "The mass of men lead lives of quiet desperation." They get up in the morning and do what they don't want to, but they won't say a thing. The old pioneer who left his home and came out here in a wagon and plowed that ground met the challenge. I admire him.

Well-designed sod-houses were warm, dry, and quiet. Some are still in use, although they may have board siding on the outside and plastered walls inside.

Left: Benton, Steve, and Charlie McCone, MN. Above: Sod-house wall.

"You Lose Another Identity of Mother Earth"

Joel Hine, an artist and musician, lives with his family in Pipestone, Minnesota. He quarries pipestone from the Pipestone National Monument area and uses it for his carvings of pipes, buffaloes, horses, bears, falcons, and other American wildlife.

"I got a permit from the monument. . . . You got to have papers—documentation that you're a Native American. I'm a Sioux Indian, full-blooded. . . .

"The Native American is in touch with Mother Earth. . . . I think we do have a sense. Myself, I love animals and respect them even down to a little grasshopper, because they were all put on this earth . . . to serve a purpose. I think all Indians have this. . . . We're all in touch together. . . . [But] there isn't much left of anything of the Indian culture, I don't think . . . , because it's so modernized. Myself, I'd like to learn the Lakota language. . . . It should be secured for the future and preserved—the language at least. . . .

"There's this one, Great-grandma Wilson, that lives in town. She's, I think, 86 or 90. She can talk Lakota. She names all the pipemakers, gives them their Indian names. . . . Hapa is my Indian name. It means 'dedication.' She can vision, you know, what kind of man you are. She can look at you, and she knows your character. She's the head of the whole Indian community around here . . . ; but she's kinda sick. Back in the olden days, when old people got sick, it was for a reason because your time was up. But now . . . they just feed her pills and stuff. I don't think that's right, to prolong life when it's just agony. . . .

"When you get to a certain age, don't you feel that you appreciate things more? Life, in general, I mean. A tree, anything. I do. When I was a kid, I used to be a major hunter. Now I won't even think of killing an animal, because it's just so senseless. An animal is so innocent. We're so superior to a dumb little animal. It's just wrong when people shoot something. That's just like committing murder, because animals don't have no defense at all. . . . [Killing the buffaloes] was terrible. That was really a slaughter. Just look at all the extinct animals now. . . . [If you lose a species], you lose another identity of Mother Earth, a very small fraction of Mother Earth that won't return ever. I want my kids to respect everything that God has given us. . . .

"For being in the 1980's, [reservation life] is real disappointing, for sure. Hopelessness, despair. . . . Nothing seems to work. The government thinks, 'Throw a few million dollars' is gonna make everyone happy. It seems like they don't funnel the money into the right programs. And people that really need it don't seem like they get it. . . . I don't think the Indian people are educated enough. . . . I don't know how to really approach the reservation dilemma, but the main thing is that it's up to the individuals that live on it. . . .

Before the Spanish reintroduced the horse upon the North American continent in the early sixteenth century, the Plains tribes lived along rivers and streams. They subsisted by gathering wild fruits, vegetables, and forbs; by fishing; and by hunting small game. Only occasionally did they hunt bison. The Dakotas discovered and began to rely upon the horse in the eighteenth century as they were driven westward by the Chippewas, who had acquired guns. Reliance on the horse made the Plains Indians more dependent on the bison for survival. In 1883 the last herds of buffalo were gone, with only a few scattered survivors.

The sacred pipestone quarry was available to American Indians for more than four hundred years. But in 1893 the Yankton-Dakotas lost control of the quarries under the law of eminent domain. A federal Indian school was constructed on the site. In 1937, an Act of Congress made the quarries again available to Indians of all tribes.

Left: Joel Hine, MN.
Above: Petroglyphs, Historic Site, MN.

"The Indian people just make a mockery out of [the missionary work]. That's what it is, honestly. They probably show kindness and all. . . . I don't think the Indian people [are without] religion, because they were already born with it and know it. . . . They got it in the blood. . . .

"When we feel like we're not in touch anymore . . . , you go to a sweat lodge. Then you take peyote. . . . We do that for spiritual reasons. Try to cleanse the soul. You got to go in there with a medicine man. . . . One of my uncles told me what kind of experience it is. You just feel more refreshed once you're done. You've got more insight on the world again. It makes you more aware, puts more awareness in your soul. Someday, I'm gonna try it myself. . . . There are certain things about Indians that are really astonishing. . . .

"There's a lot of prejudice yet. We're all stereotyped, and it gets so old. Some of these Eastern people . . . think that we're still riding horses with our spears and still hunting buffalo. I just want them to know that we got a purpose in life, too, just like everyone else. I want the American people to respect us more. . . .

"My goal in life is I want to be a representative for the Indian people through my music. There's no performing Indians in the arts. You see, I'll be the first one. I'll succeed eventually, someday."

The Minnesota pipestone is also called catlinite, after George Catlin, who explored the pipestone quarry in Minnesota in 1836. The stone lies in a thin layer, about twelve to eighteen inches, sandwiched in layers of Sioux quartzite, a much harder stone. It is believed that some 1.2 billion years ago the pipestone was clay deposited between layers of sand (the quartzite) at the bottom of a sea.

The pipe, or calumet, carved from pipestone was used by the American Indian tribes for various purposes: to show intentions for war or peace, to seal treaties or agreements (seldom broken), to solemnize an occasion, and to strengthen alliances. The legends describing the origin of the use of the calumet differ. In the Dakota or Lakota legend, the pipe is brought to the chief by White Buffalo Woman. The pipe stem is pointed toward the heavens, and power is drawn from the six directions— west, north, east, south, the sky, and the earth—calling forth the Great Spirit.

Left: Cottonwood tree.
Above: Pipestone layer.

"Oh, I Love the Birds"

Mary Sue Bihr was the first president of the garden club that originated the planting of azaleas and dogwoods in Charleston, Missouri. Each April the town holds its Azalea Festival.

"I was born next door, but I was just a little tiny girl when my family built this house, and it's the only place I can remember ever having lived except when I was married and away from home and lived in north Missouri. . . .

"[My husband] was a merchant. And my father was before him, and his father before him. My great-grandfather built the first railroad through here. . . .

"I get a lot of pleasure out of my flowers, always have. And you see, we organized a garden club here in 1954 or maybe in 1953 . . . , and really the garden club is responsible for all this beauty in Charleston. . . .

The flowering dogwood is a native tree found in the extreme eastern edges of the tallgrass prairies and on northeast to Maine. In natural woodlands the dogwood flowers are white, while cultivated dogwoods may be a showy pink. The azalea is a colorful flowering shrub.

"Well, I think [the beauty of the flowers] is spiritual. I think you feel a closeness to God. . . . And then for all this to open up right at Easter time, it just has some special meaning. . . .

"You see, cotton was king here. Charleston was a thriving town . . . , very good business-wise . . . , and now it just isn't any more.

"I can remember when these streets were paved for the first time. They had street dances to celebrate having paved streets.

"Yet through all those days, everybody here had always had a cook and a yard man, and I never saw it when we didn't have, even through the Depression. Goodness, the help! They didn't pay 'em anything, hardly. But now Lizzie did have a home here and she was part—really—part of the family. That was our cook. . . .

"I don't blame them. They don't want to be servants. They shouldn't be. Shouldn't have been—ever. It shouldn't have been. I'm careful how I say that, though; there are still some diehards. . . .

"Oh, I love the birds. . . . And the wrens. . . . You wouldn't believe it, one day I had my missionary church group of women on the porch. . . . [The wrens] were singing so loud we couldn't even hear the program."

Left: Mary Sue Bihr, MO.
Above: Dogwoods in bloom;
azaleas in bloom.

"In Bloom Now Is the Dogwood"

David Payne owns a sawmill near Fairdealing, Missouri. With two employees he produces railroad ties, pallet stock, and hardwood flooring from red oak and post oak.

David: I'm just a small mill.... Cut 'em down and cut logs to the length and drag 'em in. I just use a farm tractor to drag them in with, and then we load them on a truck and haul them into the mill.

Sometimes [business is good]. Sometimes I wish I wasn't in it.

I think we're cuttin' it all out faster than it's growin' back. They've tried to get the law passed where if anybody cuts down a tree, why, they'd have to set another one out. It never passed, though.

Hired man: What I can't understand is, when the government [clears a] tract of timber, it's clear-cut. They cut everything out of it, little trees and all.

David: [The national forest], that's what we're talkin' about . . . , the Mark Twain National Forest.

If the [Japanese] keeps on buyin' up the state, the buildings and lands . . . , they'll be our government.

Hired Man: [Our country] is on the way out. It's on the way out; we're losin' it. They're talkin' about puttin' in a big ole steel mill down there in Arkansas. Japanese steel mill they'll be puttin' in.

[To the politicians] I'd say, quit bein' so greedy.

David: [In the woods] there's turkey, deer, squirrel, rabbit, and wolfs or coyotes— whatever you call 'em. . . .

The ones in bloom now is the dogwood. I'd miss it [if it were gone]. I look at em . . . drivin' down the road or sumpthin'. Dogwood, wild plum, and the redbud . . . , there's just all kind of spring [here].

It is doubtful whether southern Missouri was ever dominated by the prairie, but its flora and fauna exemplify woodland boundaries ready to move west into the prairie. Relatively slight climatic changes, such as a global cooling trend or an increase in rainfall, would bring the forest's leading edge of oaks, sumacs, and wild plum west.

Left: David Payne, MO.
Above: Working the sawmill.

"Certainly by the Year 2200 . . ."

Dean L. Roberts, Jr., is the senior environmental coordinator for Thunder Basin Coal Company at the Black Thunder Mine near Wright, Wyoming. He has been a radiation-safety officer in a uranium mine and a county extension agent in Utah. He has a graduate degree in range management.

"I am [involved] with computer-modeling the effect that coal mining is going to have upon ground water and the air, making sure that we stay within the regulatory requirements.

"Thunder Basin Coal Company has a strong environmental program, which states that we will return the land to as good a productive state as it was before we mined it. We have a very strong environmental ethic. I think that's as it should be in order to maintain an image as a good corporate citizen of the state.

"When we talk about an environmental ethic we have to look at it in terms of distinguishing between conservation and preservation. Many environmental groups are looking at preservation as opposed to conservation. We believe that conservation is the wise use of a resource. From a personal religious viewpoint, this resource was put out here for us to use wisely or unwisely. Personally I am trying to see that it is used wisely and that we do return the prairie to a productive state.

"The Wyoming State Land Quality Division regulations require us, prior to mining, to remove all the topsoil and stockpile it. Then we remove the overburden, which is all the material above the coal. We replace [all this] after the coal is mined. . . . So in essence we remove the coal seam and then put everything back the way it was before. Then we provide habitat for wildlife, including the small animals such as the ground squirrels, antelope, a few elk, and also provide for use by livestock. [When we're done] we've just lowered everything by the thickness of the coal seam, around sixty-five feet.

"In terms of using the resource as opposed to preserving it for a later time, I have faith in mankind that technology will replace coal. Coal, oil, and natural gas are sources of energy which will be used up at some point in time, certainly oil and natural gas much sooner than coal. By the last estimate I heard there are two hundred years' worth of coal energy [left] in the United States. But certainly by the year 2200 immense strides [in energy technology] are going to be made.

The Black Thunder coal mine is a surface mine; the work is done above the earth's surface. A layer of soil and overburden fifteen to three hundred feet thick is removed to expose the coal, which is excavated by huge electric shovels and hauled to coal crushers. The haul trucks have a load capacity of 170 tons. The mine produces about twenty million tons of sub-bituminous low-sulphur coal annually.

The viewpoint that natural resources exist for human consumption and pleasure is known as an anthropocentric perspective. An ecocentric position assumes that all inhabitants of a biotic community have inherent citizenship privileges, independent of their value to people.

Left: Dean L. Roberts, Jr., WY. Above: Elk.

"Technology will advance to a point to where the source of energy will be something other than coal, whether it is the sun, or we harness the winds, or whether we use a fusion as opposed to a fission nuclear process. Something is going to take place. I think fusion will eventually happen.

"My life is based around my family and around my religion, and from a religious point of view I think that God provided resources to be used. Stewardship requires us to use a resource properly, to provide for the welfare of all, to provide for cheap electrical generation so that we can assist the poor. . . .

"Looking at it from a family point of view, I'm trying to teach my children that a resource is there to be used as opposed to being preserved. We do need areas [where] we can go to see things as they used to be, but it certainly does not need to be as extreme as is being proposed by certain groups.

"I think every person needs to have a small piece of ground where they can grow a flower and go out and get their hands dirty. We can't create a flower. We can't create an antelope. We can observe and enjoy. . . ."

Unit trains of about a hundred cars, each car carrying a hundred tons, haul the coal to generating plants in Texas, Oklahoma, Kansas, Wisconsin, and Nebraska. An average of six mile-long trains leave the mine daily. While loading, the train moves through the loading shed at four miles per hour.

Nuclear fission generates electricity by splitting uranium and plutonium atoms, creating highly radioactive by-products. It is believed that nuclear fusion, in which the nuclei of a light element are transformed into those of a heavier element, would yield much more energy with less waste at a lower radiation level. Scientists are working to control the explosive energy of the fusion process.

Left: Common sagebrush. Above: Jack rabbit.

"You Get this Eerie Feeling"

Sandy Wilson is a bone preservationist at the Mammoth Site of Hot Springs, South Dakota. She injects a preservative into the fossil bones of giant Columbian mammoths as they are meticulously unearthed where they died more than twenty-six thousand years ago. The skeletal remains of two mammoths have been nicknamed Marie and Napoleon.

"The mammoth bones were discovered in 1974. At the time, I lived only about four blocks from here, so it was really exciting. . . . When they first uncovered the bones, the man that was doing the bulldozing stopped because he kept taking off chunks of a tusk. That evening, he had his son, who was a geology student at Chadron [Nebraska] State College, come up and look.

"We feel that the mammoths were here, wandering in herds through the prairie. They wanted to come in here to drink or to bathe, to swim; and, not realizing how treacherous the banks of the pond were, would wander down . . . and not be able to come back up. The red shale was just like ice when it was wet, and they would become entrapped.

"Many [other] mammoth finds, of course, have been [associated] with man. They found [spear] points with them and so on. But this site being twenty-six thousand years old, [paleontologists] don't feel that man was here at that time.

"The adult animals were probably between twelve and fifteen feet tall at the shoulder. They estimate these animals could have weighed more than ten tons, the males, and the females being a little bit less, maybe between six and eight tons. The mammoths could eat up to five hundred pounds of grass in a day.

"We have found evidence of other animals being present at the same time. We found the teeth of an ice-age camel, of a gray wolf, and a peccary. They found some of the bones of the short-faced bear. That was a major find in 1983. . . . He stood about six feet tall at the shoulders, standing on all fours. . . . He weighed about fifteen hundred pounds, but we believe he was very fast.

"My kids are really excited about the mammoth dig. My boy is going to be eleven this summer. He's into the fossils, dinosaurs and all of that. I try to relate . . . the span of time, how much newer these animals are than the dinosaurs. We could relate the [dinosaur age], sixty-five million years ago, to when the Black Hills and the Rocky Mountains were uplifted. The mammoths are fairly new. They came across the Bering land bridge many years ago, one-and-one-half million years ago, and survived until about eleven thousand years ago.

The Mammoth Site of Hot Springs, a graveyard for huge Pleistocene elephants, is located at the south edge of South Dakota's Black Hills. As many as a hundred Columbian mammoths may have slipped into a steep-sided pond here during the last ice age and drowned. Now their fossil remains are being meticulously excavated and preserved by Earthwatch volunteers every summer. The huge bones, skulls, and tusks are carefully exposed with trowels, dental picks, and brushes, but left in place so people can readily see what happened. Forty-one mammoth skeletons have been identified.

The largest living land animal native to the prairie is the bison, commonly called buffalo. Large males may stand six feet tall at the shoulders and weigh over a ton. Bison can gallop over thirty miles per hour, and they are good swimmers. Both sexes have short, curved horns. The gestation period is about 280 days, and the calves, usually born in May, are red at birth and through the first summer. The life span is about twenty-five years.

Left: Sandy Wilson, SD. Above: Mammoth skull, "Napoleon."

"I seem to have a very strong attachment to what has happened here. To try to relate, trying to put yourself back into that time period, you almost have to start daydreaming. You think about the large numbers of these animals and how huge they were, wandering across this prairie. Then to have a burial site of these animals, a natural death-trap situation.... You begin to feel an attachment to the animals, almost personally, when you work on them. When I'm up by Marie doing bone preservation, the way that she's lying on her left side in mud, you can just almost see the animal.... You get this really eerie feeling because you can see these long leg bones and these huge ribs, and you can see the mud taking the place of where this animal's belly used to be. It's almost as if this animal could stand up.... It's just a feeling that you can't describe.

"Tell [the public] to come visit the Mammoth Site of Hot Springs. Whether you're young or old, you can come here and you're going to learn something. You're going to walk away with your own theories, your own ideas of what happened. I think people really need to feel what's happened in the past, to be able to look at something and realize that this really happened, this isn't just a structure set up in Hot Springs with a bunch of bones that have been placed in the ground. It was a natural death trap. I mean, these animals died and were buried as the years went by....

"I said [to a creationist], 'We did not put these bones here. God did this. Man cannot do this sort of thing on his own.' I said, 'I'm a Christian, too. And this is here, this is evidence of the past....'"

"Buffalo ranching" is becoming quite common due to buffalo meat's low fat and low cholesterol content. Beef contains ninety-nine calories per ounce, while buffalo meat has thirty-eight calories. The cholesterol content is twenty-five percent lower than that of beef.

Large predators—grizzly bears, mountain lions, and gray wolves—were necessary links in the prairie environment to limit the population of herbivorous animals such as bison, deer, elk, and other grass-eaters. At one time these animals ranged over the entire prairie region, but most prairie-dwelling carnivores were destroyed after settlers arrived. Today these animals are found only in the mountains west of the prairie states.

Left: Sunrise reflection.
Above: Two bison bulls.

"There's No End to the Universe"

Nine-year-old Jason Perry spent part of his summer vacation in Clayton, New Mexico. A participant in his school's gifted program, he writes poetry, composes music, and paints. Jason is interested in science, especially dinosaurs, astronomy, electronics, and the space program. He and his family live in Wolf City, Texas. His mother, Paula, is a registered nurse. His father, Leslie, is a firefighter.

"A poem? Okay. It's called 'Dinosaurs.' 'Dinosaurs lived long ago./ And when they fought,/ It was a fantastic show./ Dinosaurs are reptiles, see,/ And some would even eat me.'

"I heard about [dinosaurs] one day; and then, I started getting interested, reading more and more about 'em, and then, finally, I was just so interested, they became my favorite type [of animal]. I was in [preschool]. . . .

"I saw some [dinosaur] tracks at the park [near Clayton] in this kind of rock stuff . . . , and there were some [different] kinds, like the sauropods, the round foot. . . . If there weren't [dinosaurs], what tracks would there be, and what bones? They've gotta be giant animals, and we just named them dinosaurs, or terrible lizards. . . .

"Dinosaurs are reptiles [but] not lizards. Some people think they were all warm-blooded, like birds. They had small brains. Some of them, like the stegosaurus, had a brain as small as a walnut. . . .

"I think about 125 million years ago the first dinosaur arose. I think it was [in] . . . the Triassic period. There were shell-headed fish, you know—I don't know the word for them—and then there were smaller lizards. [There were] giant things of what we now know today, like scorpions, giant spiders, giant mosquitos, horseflies, dragonflies, and especially giant trees. That's what the biggest plant-eaters lived on. . . .

"One day, when I watched [the movie] *Back to the Future*, I just kept drawing some cars that [go back in time]. And I started drawing other machines after I read another book about this man who builds a time machine and goes back to the dinosaur age. Then, that's what I wanted to do. When I get there, first I'm gonna have to build a suit, so when they step on me they'll pass right through me like a ghost. Then I'm gonna capture one of their eggs; and when I bring it back, I'm gonna help it adapt to the new changes of the world. I won't do that for the fame, the fortune, or the money, or anything. I just want to do it. Scientists don't know everything about dinosaurs, and I can say more about dinosaurs than the librarian back in Wolf City can. . . .

"I like to paint dinosaurs, but there's no book that says how. . . . One of them had some dinosaur pictures in it. . . . But I could tell on the first page it wasn't true, because the brontosaurus, or whatever sauropod it was, had like stick legs. . . .

"On this vacation, so far, I've read two books, and pretty thick ones, too. One is *The Hobbit*, the beginning story of *The Lord of the Rings*, and one of them was *Star Trek II.*

Dinosaurs appeared in the oldest period of the Mesozoic era, the Triassic, from two hundred million to 140 million years ago and died out in the Cretaceous period. The word dinosaur *(from the Greek* dino, *meaning* terrible, *and* saurus, *meaning* lizard*) is applied to two different groups of reptiles, saurischians, having typical reptile hips, and ornithischians, having bird-like hips.*

More than five hundred dinosaur footprints lie in the Cretaceous sandstone at Clayton Lake State Park in New Mexico. One set of tracks was made by the "handprints" of a pterodactyl, a flying creature. Another set is from a web-footed dinosaur.

New climatic variations that marked the Late Cretaceous and Early Cenozoic periods created zones for plants and set the stage for animals to evolve. The angiosperms, flowering plants including grasses, appeared in the Early Cretaceous period and spread rapidly across drier climates. With the age of flowers came the age of mammals.

Left: Jason Perry vacationing, NM. Above: Dinosaur track.

"[The mammoths and mastodons] lived in the ice-age period. That's probably why the dinosaurs died—[because] the ice age began. . . . That was one of my theories. My second, I have two theories, comets and meteors have crashed on this earth. A giant one crashed into—there's this giant crater somewhere in Arizona—exactly there and sent radioactive rays all around the planet, killing all the dinosaurs.

"The cave man [came on the scene] . . . about two million years ago—the Neanderthal man, and . . . something called the "cave bear." It was a giant bear. I only read about it in a small part in one of my books. . . .

"I'm trying to get a job right now, doing some stuff like lumbering, working stuff. I have this imaginary job that I don't like to discuss. . . .

"I'm gonna be a scientist. . . . One day I'm gonna build spaceships; and I'm gonna just build a science station where all my science friends work. I'm gonna join the Air Force, then be a scientist. I'm gonna go out in outer space, you know, like on Star Trek. I'm gonna build this kinda beaming thing, so I can go out somewhere, beyond the Large Clouds, and I can go out of the galaxy. . . . There's no end to [the universe], some people say. . . .

"I don't know why, but some people think that others are just weird, because—like skin coloring and . . . sometimes just their language. . . . They speak a certain language, and people think they're queer. I think that everyone should be considered equal. . . .

"And that's another thing. When people are smart and go to another grade, and they're younger, everybody teases them, saying, 'I don't like you,' or stuff. . . .

"I don't think any animal should become extinct. Everything has its own part in nature. I just don't like anything to become extinct."

The fossil remains of the oldest known member of the genus Homo *have been dated to a million years ago.* Homo erectus *existed in the early Middle Pleistocene, one million to five hundred thousand years ago. Modern man belongs to the species* Homo sapiens. *The Neanderthal fossil dates between Middle and Upper Pleistocene or from one hundred thousand to thirty-five thousand years ago. Cro-Magnon, strictly speaking the oldest modern man, emerged approximately thirty-five thousand years ago.*

Thirty-five years ago space travel was a dream. In 1961, a Russian, Yuri Gagarin, became the first space traveler and the first person to orbit the earth. In 1962, aboard Mercury 6, John Glenn became the first American to orbit the earth. As of January 1, 1988, 201 people had completed one or more orbits of the earth. In 1976 two American Viking spacecraft landed on Mars, and in 1981 the U. S. launched the first space shuttle. In 1986 Voyager 2 (U.S.A.) flew past Uranus. By the year 10,000,000, Voyager 2 may drift into another solar system.

Left: Jason, Paula and Leslie Perry. Above: Cholla bloom.

"Feelings, Bordering on Religion"

L. L. Males is president of the Security State Bank in Cheyenne, Oklahoma. In the mid-1930's, he led in developing the concept of upstream watershed projects for flood control and conservation in Oklahoma. His first project, Sandstone Creek, was a model for federal watershed projects.

"What got us started in watershed development? Well, like I say, I grew up on a farm and worked in the bank as a janitor. That was in 1924. When the man that ran the bank, a Mr. Hunt, quit, I was just a kid, but they left me to run the bank. And in '34 we had wind erosion and water erosion that wouldn't quit, and so I got interested in trying to stop that. I conceived the idea that the bank, instead of buying calendars, would buy transits and terracing equipment.

"But what really brought the watershed thing to life ..., in '34 we had the terrible flood on the [Washita] River. The Washita's right north of town. Thirty people were drowned. It just ruined the bottom land and the bridges and everything like a flood would. So we thought then that something had to be done.

"Dr. Black from Washington, from the Department of Agriculture, came out and visited for a few days. [We] went over south of Amarillo ... to a lake that had been built over there. He was the one that ... finished my [watershed] idea. Pretty quick after that, the concept of the watershed program was discovered or created by the Department of Agriculture.

"The people from Washington got a number of us enthused about it, so we organized the Washita River program. Our Sandstone Creek was the first one to get all of the easements and all of the structures. It took several years, because the war came along. Stopped it all.... [The project] was finished in '53 ..., twenty-three structures on 65 thousand acres.

"When we got it completed we had visitors from every place in this country, and a lot from overseas. Oklahoma didn't serve black people in our restaurants and things. First time we ever felt free to take a black person to a restaurant was when we were taking these people from various foreign countries, who had some black people in the group, to the restaurants here. That sounds ancient now. That's how recent the silly thing was. In the fifties and the sixties, it was common.

"But back to the watershed program.... Oh, my goodness, it was a matter of survival. These rains were washing our land away and the dust bowl [was blowing] it away.... Without much imagination, you could see the churches, the schools, the villages and towns, and the bank go down the river. We couldn't go on like that.

Before the prairie land was plowed, soils rich in humus and protected by grass absorbed most of the rainwater, which was slowly filtered into nearby streams. The result was a fairly even stream flow throughout the year.

Since farming had reduced the soil's ability to absorb water and accelerated erosion, the Sandstone Creek project helped restore stability to stream-flow patterns on Sandstone Creek.

An upstream watershed project goes a step beyond usual conservation practices. Watershed structures impound excess runoff for a planned period of time to prevent downstream flooding. Regular conservation techniques, such as terraces, waterways, and minumum tillage, are prerequisites for land draining into a watershed structure.

Left: L. L. Males, OK. Above: Chinaberry tree fruit.

"I was thinking about myself, my children, and other people. I didn't think about the wildlife; we didn't think about it in the beginning. Now when the land was settled, there were turkeys and deer. . . . But the homesteaders took care of that; they had to live on them.

"It all goes together: conservation, number one; watershed treatment, number two. [I have] very deep feelings, bordering on religion, about all this. It benefits everybody. I don't think it's fair to say that the farmer has to pay for all of it, because he can't.

"There was a time when the soil conservation people were all evangelists. The guys that ran these county offices and things, they just went out and made a believer out of you."

A watershed structure is an earthen dam constructed across a small stream to hold back water in a temporary reservoir. Drawdown tubes are designed to release water from this reservoir at a rate safe for the downstream channel capacity. Usually a small permanent pool remains for livestock and wildlife watering purposes. These permanent pools may range in size from a few acres to several hundred acres. The primary purpose of an upstream watershed program is to retain as much rainwater as possible in the area where it falls.

Most of the economic benefits of a watershed structure accrue to properties downstream in the form of decreased siltation, flood prevention, and stabilized stream flow. Fishing and hunting are extra benefits. Watershed costs are usually shared by governmental bodies with the owners of the structure sites.

Left: Redbud tree.
Above: Soil profile.

"That's a Bunch of Bull"

Ranch hand Curtis Wyatt and his wife live on the Shamburger Ranch in the northwest corner of Texas. Their nearest neighbors live four miles west. The closest shopping center is in Dalhart, forty-two miles south. Remnants of the defunct XIT ranch are close to the Wyatt home. Except for trees at the nearby natural spring, called Buffalo Springs, the countryside is a grass plain.

"I take care of all the cattle . . . , me and my son. We generally run between two and three thousand yearlings and between six and seven hundred mother cows.

"Twenty to twenty-five head to the section is what we try to carry. We're under-stocked. That-a-way you don't get in a bind if you have a dry summer or something. We have fifty-five sections that belong to the ranch and we have two lease sections. . . . Part of this ranch is on the old XIT Ranch and part of it's not.

"The native grasses are buffalo grass and side oats and grama grass predominantly. Some of these [irrigation] circles have been [replanted] into the [Conservation Reserve Program]. . . . They're not grazable yet. . . . Ten years . . . , that's the government program. . . .

"There's a lot of our country was homesteaded . . . over towards Texline . . . , plowed up. A lot of that Rita Blanca [National Grassland] was old homesteads. Now in the Dust Bowl days . . . , way back there . . . , the people just pulled up and went off and left, and the government took [the land] over. [Now] it's government land . . . leased to small farmers.

"We've got one section in New Mexico and we've got about five or six sections in Oklahoma that belong to us. Everything else is in Texas. . . .

"We use horses to gather all of our cattle and to do the brandin' and that sort of thing and to move them from pasture to pasture. We've got our own mares and our own stallion and we raise our own horses. Now I have a son in Dalhart that breaks them for us. . . .

"Yes, the pronghorn is definitely a nuisance. They can tear up more fences than you can fix in a month. . . . They'll go under them, and when they do, they tear the wire and knock the 'steeples' out of the post and stretch the wires. A deer will jump the fence. And [the pronghorn] graze wheat. . . . We've had as many as 150 in one bunch. I think they should be preserved. They're part of our heritage, but like I said they're a nuisance. [We also have] coyotes, bobcats, and coons and porcupines. . . .

The federal Conservation Reserve Program (CRP) is designed to stabilize farm production and encourage land conservation practices. The program requires farmers to put certain lands into grass for ten years. In exchange, the government compensates the farmer for lost income. The program's premise is that conservation is of vital importance to everyone and that the cost must be shared.

Between the late 1800's and the end of World War I, various federal homestead and land settlement provisions encouraged people to settle on prairie lands. Most programs were beneficial, but some in the High Plains were ill-advised. Land was broken up in areas where rainfall was often insufficient to produce crops. In the Dust Bowl era the federal government repurchased some of the land to bring it back to grass. These areas are known as the National Grasslands.

Left: Curtis Wyatt, TX.
Above: Buffalo Springs, TX.

"This ranch had no farming at all, except our alfalfa, until 1970, when we started irrigating and plowing up fields. A lot of people did, and they plowed up land that shouldn'ta ever had a plow put in it. And it blowed away and some of it was a disaster. . . . This government [CRP] program come along, so we put it back to grass. I think if it wasn't for the government programs there'd be a lot of farmers huntin' jobs. . . .

"I hear all these people talking 'bout . . . , oh, they can't get a job, they can't do this, and they can't do that. Well, I think that's a bunch of bull. You might have to get a job shoveling manure somewhere, but you can find a job. You might not like it, and you may not be makin' fifty cents an hour but I'd rather be makin' fifty cents an hour than settin' on my butt doin' nothin'. . . .

"[When it snows] it's a son of a gun; our driveway is four miles long. The last little blizzard we had, I got stuck trying to get out. . . . We have a big dozer blade on this four-wheel-drive Steiger. . . . I just radioed. . . .

"Everybody that works here is a family man. We've got the manager's house up there, and then we have four more houses [for the other workers], and I live down yonder, where those trees are."

The pronghorn, once declining in population, has made a comeback. There are estimated to be half a million. Hunting is necessary in most shortgrass prairie states to control their numbers, since natural predators, such as wolves, are scarce. The pronghorn can run up to seventy miles per hour.

Left: Prickly pear cactus.
Above: Pronghorn.

"Tighten Your Belt and Quit Spending"

Earl W. Scott and his son, Earl Jr., operate the Canon Land and Livestock Company, a sheep and cattle operation headquartered in Douglas, Wyoming. This grassland and farmland covers 373 sections in Converse County. Most of the land is owned, although some is leased from the state of Wyoming, the Bureau of Land Management, the National Grasslands, and private owners.

"This ranch and it's predecessor are an old, old ranch established within this area in about 1890 by John Morton. . . . He died in 1916, and his wife and son took this ranch over. . . .

"Mrs. Morton, Sarah Morton, was a true businesswoman. . . . She owned half the town of Douglas at one time, including the electric power plant. . . .

"The worst injustice [the federal government] ever gave the World War I veterans was to give them 640 acres of land and send them out here to make a living on it. It was impossible. And those people stayed in here and I mean they basically starved to death for that period through the 1920's. And they left, left their equipment, left everything on the ground and just took out. . . .

"Well, the National Grasslands are the outgrowth of the Depression in the thirties. These homesteaders left this country. All they wanted was enough money to get out of it. They were starving to death. [The federal government] bought all this stuff up as inferior land.

"This particular outfit that I'm with bought a lot of land in the 1930's. They had a standard price for purchase, a dollar an acre . . . , the same price the government was paying.

"There isn't any question in my mind [that ranching is the proper usage for this land]. Anybody who has been in the ranching business as long as this ranch has operated has not mismanaged or abused the ground or they wouldn't be here today.

"I do think that all land in the United States needs to be used. I'm strongly in favor of the multiple-use concept. . . . I am deadly opposed to wilderness land per se. Well, they set this aside and there's probably one one-hundredth in our population that ever get an opportunity to use that. There are very few people who can backpack in there. . . .

"As a rancher I feel I'm a conservationist. But I'm not an environmentalist as it exists today. I may be telling you something that you don't want to hear. . . .

"Well, in today's economy [pesticides and chemicals] probably are a necessary thing, but I think it definitely has to be controlled. I think there have to be strong regulations. . . . Your pesticides, your various chemicals and commercial fertilizer, I think, are deteriorating our ground step by step. But, when you take that all away, [the land] deteriorates right now.

The National Grasslands, encompassing thousands of acres in most shortgrass states, are a mystery to travelers. Road maps display the Grasslands, but the countryside has no sign posts pointing them out. There are no gateways, visitor centers, or guided trails.

The Grasslands were purchased from financially distressed ranchers and farmers in the Dust Bowl era. Originally homesteaded at the turn of the century, the land was plowed to meet homestead requirements. We now realize that it was too arid for crop cultivation. Ranchers now are leasing this land, while the U. S. government regulates usage.

Left: Earl W. Scott, WY. Above: Range cattle.

"I think erosion needs to be controlled . . . , but I'm not going to say the government should do that.

"The canal we irrigate out of was started in the late 1880's. . . . [It starts] nine miles above the ranch out of the North Platte. They talk of taking the waters away from the whooping crane and all that sort of thing. Wyoming is not taking that water away. That water is being taken away by pumps . . . in Nebraska itself.

"I will say that sheep are survivors. . . . They are very well oriented to winter weather. And you get two money crops off of them each year. You get a wool crop. You get a lamb. And we can co-mingle them with cattle.

"To me the sheep industry has been the lifeline of the Wyoming livestock industry. . . .

"Rustling? Yes, we have had in the past. Today we have a range detective . . . I would say he's part Indian. He lives like an Indian. He's out and prowls all night.

"[About hard times I would say], tighten your belt and quit spending money. That's the whole thing. . . . You've got to change your lifestyle. . . .

"Well, getting back to nature, that is one of the greatest things that is in anyone's philosophy. And I don't think anybody has lived until they get back there, visit with the birds, watch wild animals. . . . It's a thing you can't buy anywhere for money. It's that simple. Aloneness is good for you. . . .

"Oh, there isn't any question about it. You bet, you have to be a survivor to stay out here."

While the Grasslands are not identified along the highways, an alert traveler can watch for old plow furrows, fence lines, and a difference in the grass. Often a derelict windmill, rusty tin grain bins, or a house and barn abandoned to raccoons and owls may mark a farmstead. Wheat-farming equipment of threshing-machine vintage, abandoned fifty years ago, seems out of context in range country.

Sheep ranching is a major industry in the range country of Wyoming. Sheep range land at the Canon Cattle Company is divided by fences so that herders are not required. Earl Scott claims that sheep will equalize their grazing over an area if they are free to roam. With a herdsman, sheep were bunched up, overgrazing in one spot. Sheep are better adapted than cattle to the harsh, arid Wyoming climate. Annual wool and lamb crops offer diversity to the rancher.

*Left: Range sheep.
Above: Abandoned one-way plow.*

"It's Either the Colors or the Music"

Botanist Cynthia Reed is the director of the planned Claude A. Barr Memorial Botanical Garden at the Mammoth Site of Hot Springs, South Dakota. Ms. Reed was a neighbor of Claude Barr, a self-educated botanist who discovered several species of Great Plains flowers before he died in 1982. The botanical garden will emphasize plants native to the American Great Plains.

"For a while it was very stylish among people in the East to be concerned about the American Southwest. . . . There were people who did a lot to elevate [concern for the Southwest] in the consciousness of the stylish people. And that is one of the things that needs to be done for the prairie.

"That's the justification for the [Claude Barr] Botanical Garden. There are botanic gardens all over the United States focusing on every geographical, geological area except the prairies.

"I think that every area, whether it's the jungle or whether it's the desert, can be appreciated, but it must be appreciated for what it is and studied. . . .

"I feel [that the prairie] is a major portion of our continent, and I think we have a responsiblity to understand and preserve all the variety that God put on the earth, because we in our omnipotence . . . don't understand the complex interactions. For us to arrogantly disregard all the unknown factors of an area and totally destroy it is the height of irresponsibility.

"I came from a ranch out in the middle of the western half of South Dakota. My parents, grandparents, and great-grandparents lived there since before this was a state. I guess [the prairie has] gotten into our blood. But we like the sky. We like to be able to breathe air. We like to see the flowers and the birds and the coyotes and all.

"We have an ongoing debate in our families—a little humorous debate—over why it is we live here . . . , because clearly it is not the money. So we've decided it's either the colors or the music. And that's because if you really just open your eyes and look, it must be the colors. The sunsets are incredible, and the colors of the terrain.

"And yet sometimes if you're driving down the road and you hear a meadowlark, it zings in your ear. Then you think it's not the colors, it's the music. Because the music is pretty good, too—just the birds, the insects, the sounds that you can hear.

"I have a network of friends and relatives that, it doesn't matter where we are or what time of the night it is, if we see the northern lights we phone [each other] and say, 'Go outside and see if you can see them.' Sometimes even if we are two hundred miles apart we can go and look and—it's funny the different things we'll see—we're both seeing the northern lights. . . .

"A lot of the rewards and I'm sure a lot of the reason people live on grasslands [involve] the real abstract psychological feeling that they get simply from being able to see far horizons, from having the big open sky over them and from having a lot of good old 1940's western songs always saying that kind of thing. . . .

The one million square miles of the Prairie Bioregion that stretches over central North America contains a rich variety of grasses and forbs. Ethnobotany is the study of how these plants were used by the Native Americans and early settlers for food and medicinal purposes.

Much of the history of plant usage by the Native American is lost, partly because of little contact between European settlers and Indian women, who were the gatherers; and also because of the Indians' expatriation to new areas. Still, some documentation is available.

The development of flowering plants like those that cover the prairie bioregions on this planet preceded the emergence of man. Because of geological formations, climatic conditions, and the preservation ethic of the American Indian, the Prairie Bioregion in North America is unique. It was nearly treeless because of the grazing habits of elk, bison, and antelope, and because of fires set by Indians or started by lightning. Large expanses of prairie bioregions—in their true wildness—are rare. There are no National Prairie parks.

Left: Cynthia Reed, SD. Above: Yucca flower.

"The plains and the prairies are so much less studied..., less well documented than some of your other areas such as the deserts in the Southwest.... The studies that have been done here have been economically oriented. More than one person has told me that there are many species of plants yet to be identified in the grasslands.... Claude Barr trained himself in botany, and he is credited with the discovery of several varieties and one species....

"I find that people generally have a hard time understanding the vast amount of acreage that it would take to actually support a prairie [preserve].... You have to have five thousand acres before you'll be able to really have a prairie....

"As science goes on we are learning that a lot of valuable medicines lie out [in the prairie] in those plants that we haven't even named yet. The example is frequently given about the rain forest, but the same thing can easily be true of plants in the prairies.... The Native American usages of plants are very poorly documented. Some of those usages were valid. I read a story about aspirin. The willow bark that the Indians ground is the same thing as aspirin. The man [that created aspirin] in the laboratory was really trying to copy the willow bark. I am starting to see more interest in things like ethnobotany....

"I'm personally concerned about plowing or putting other tools into a topsoil. That's what affects the range of species that can survive. There are few species that can survive in subsoil, and then there are the species that have to build the topsoil, so that the other [species]—five hundred years later—may come in."

Ten percent of the twenty-two thousand U.S. native-plant species are endangered or threatened. A surprising number of these are from the Prairie Bioregion.

*Claude A. Barr began ranching in South Dakota in 1910, calling his government homestead the Prairie Gem Ranch. He studied the wildflowers of the Great Plains and established a garden of prairie flowers. He became a recognized authority in the world of botany, discovering a species of milkvetch (*Astragalus barii*) and making significant studies of* Penstemon baydenii *(blowout bluebells), which have been nominated for endangered-species status in Nebraska. His study of wildflowers is documented in his book,* Jewels of the Plains.

Left: Maximilian sunflower. Above: Corral at Reed Ranch, SD.

SCORE™ ROTARY ENGINES

In 1984, John Deere acquired all rotary engine assets, patents and technologies from Curtiss-Wright. Since then, John Deere has been actively developing the SCORE rotary engine with support from both the military and private sectors.

The SCORE (Stratified Charge Omnivorous Rotary Engine) families of engines offer a power range of 80-2250 horsepower in very compact, low-profile designs. The patented stratified charge injection system allows these engines to use a wide range of fuels, by themselves, or in any combination. Considered to be the next generation of power for land, sea and air applications, some SCORE rotary engines are slated for production in 1988.

43

"We're Looking at New Machines"

Rich Johnson is a senior scientist at the John Deere Technical Center in Moline, Illinois.

"I grew up on a grain-and-livestock farm in northwest Iowa, and went to school at Iowa State University and the University of Minnesota. I came to Deere in 1980 [as an agronomist]. Agronomists at Deere work with engineering in terms of designing machines from what we call a functional standpoint. We also work with corporate management in terms of long-term planning and trends in agriculture. . . .

"I think of [this land originally] as large expanses of grass varying from dryland on the slopes of Colorado to the almost swampy-type prairies in central Illinois and parts of Indiana. Today, particularly in Iowa and Illinois, I think of it as farmland. The soils and climate mix so well that they are prime agricultural land. The prairie just largely disappeared. . . .

"Crop yields are going up in almost all the major crops we grow, particularly in the prairies. One exception might be cotton. Corn's been advancing at the rate of about 2.2 bushels a year for the last thirty-five years now. Soybeans have been going up at about one third of a bushel a year ever since they started growing them in the 1920's. . . . So getting a machine to operate at its optimum in some of these crops is becoming a much greater challenge.

"Another major change in our business in the last fifteen or twenty years is the issue of conservation tillage . . . , making machines to handle more crop residue and to help keep that crop residue on the soil surface. In some cases, we're looking at whole new machines. . . .

"So what we're seeing in our conservation-tillage movement is a diversification of tillage methods coming in. In the early prairie years when you were going to seed something you started with the moldboard plow. Well, now we're seeing that tillage-practice syndrome getting just about as site-specific as the fertilizer and herbicide practices. That's been a real challenge to us, from a machine standpoint, to make the machines that can do these diverse things and at a cost that [farmers] can afford. . . .

"We're really concerned about contaminating our ground water with nitrates and pesticides. I think this has brought some balance back into looking at the whole ecological system of farming, and I think it's good. For a while we had people say, 'We're going to no-till everything because that's the ultimate in controlling erosion.' But then you're strictly dependent on chemicals and, in many cases, higher rates of chemicals. You can actually get into an O.D. situation on chemicals.

The tallgrass prairie has undergone a greater ecological transformation than the mixed-grass and short-grass prairies because of its fertile soil, abundance of minerals, adequate rainfall, and waterways and lakes. Thriving agriculture and industry have replaced the prairie grasses and animals.

Big bluestem and Indian grass usually predominated in the tallgrass prairie, complemented by small bluestem, switch grass, a variety of cool-season grasses, and a seasonal variation of flowering forbs. Prairie cordgrass was found in the wetter areas. Corn does well wherever big bluestem used to grow.

Left: Richard P. Johnson, IL. Above: Big bluestem and Maximilian sunflowers.

"I think most farmers are very ecologically minded. They live on that land, and they want to preserve. I think the farmer is not quite as single-issue-oriented as some [who] tend to only see chemicals, or soil erosion, or pesticides. He has to look at the whole system. I think in the long term the economics factor usually wins out. . . .

"Our view is that the portable fuels will be around in agriculture in our current design life or design cycle. We think that in the future petroleum reserves will eventually come to an end. We're blessed with tremendous coal reserves, and you can gasify coal. We're doing work with rotary engines now that will burn multiple kinds of fuel, from ethanol-type fuels . . . to vegetable oils like sunflower oil and soybean oil. . . . It's not beyond comprehension to think that in a hundred years you might have a nuclear engine running in an automobile or a tractor or a combine. . . .

"We've got almost sixty million acres of mowed turf in the United States, [about the same as] the hay crop in our country. . . . We put a lot of chemicals on [lawns]. When I was in graduate school at Ames they were looking for 2,4-D in the atmosphere, and they ran surveys of the Midwest and do you know where they found the most 2,4-D? Over every city there was a cloud of 2,4-D. You know, everybody was pegging the farmer."

The Kansas Flint Hills, thousands of acres of range land, are the only large tract of unbroken tallgrass prairie remaining. An underlying layer of rock discourages farming. The Konza Prairie, an 8,616-acre tract owned by the Nature Conservancy, is a large prairie laboratory administered by Kansas State University.

Lawns and other landscaping features consume twelve percent of all fertilizers and over one third of all pesticides used in our country. Natural prairie landscaping with native species greatly reduces the need for maintenance, fertilizers, and pesticides.

*Left: Harvest's end.
Above: Iowa cornfield.*

"I'm Awestruck by It All"

Duane Vonada owns and operates a family farm in north central Kansas. His hobby, shared with his brother, Delmar, and his son, Damon, is cutting post rock (used from 1875 to 1940 for fence posts and buildings) from the Greenhorn rock formation near Sylvan Grove.

"Our farm is about 3,700 total acres. We have a family corporation. We are all family members that operate it. We have no hired men. Damon has had two years at Hutchinson [Community College]. My daughter, Denette, an ag. econ. major, [does] the bookkeeping, financial statements, and cash flows. She operates a computer. Nowadays we're doing a lot of hedging.... I am awestruck by it all....

"I started [cutting post rock] in '76 during the centennial [celebration] because it was the heritage of this country. Then people kept requesting, 'Would you show us how you split the post rock out?' [The post-rock formation] runs from about the Nebraska line to Dodge City, about sixty miles wide. It is the only region in the United States where this rock is found. [The post-rock layer] runs between eight and fourteen inches [thick].

"Most people are amazed when they see the fossils [in the post rock]. The idea of this being a sea really amazes me—that we had an inland sea here at one time.

"I think [people] need to understand what our forefathers went through when they came out into this country in 1875. These immigrants were from Czechoslovakia and Norway and had worked with stone in their [native] countries. When they found this stone, they began to quarry it out to build their homes and make fence posts....

"The original old [rock drill] had rotted down.... I picked up the iron parts ... and reconstructed it from memory. This was what my father had—a personal invention. I don't think you could find a stone drill from a factory or buy the same one anybody else had. They were all made by local blacksmiths, farmers, or masons....

"[Delmar] has the feathers and wedges in place [in the holes we drilled], and he is driving them down tight. He's listening to the ring of each wedge to tell how tight it is. He wants each one [to have] equal tension. [The stone weighs] about 125 pounds a cubic foot—anywhere from two hundred to three hundred pounds a post....

"[Farming] is really hard and long hours. But I think what I like ... is going out and looking at our livestock and seeing the beautiful sunsets. Or just getting up in the morning—our kitchen window looks east—and seeing the sunrise every morning."

The Greenhorn rock formation is a series of thinly laminated beds consisting mostly of limestone and chalky shale deposited during the Cretaceous period, sixty million to 140 million years ago, when dinosaurs reached their apex and began their decline. The Fencepost limestone bed is the top layer. Fossils of clams, worm burrows, ammonites, fish remains (especially shark teeth), and oysters can be found there.

Many churches and other buildings have been constructed from the Fencepost limestone. The most well-known church is the Cathedral of the Plains, St. Fidelis Church in Victoria, Kansas. Picken Hall, the administration building at Fort Hays State College in Hays, Kansas, is also built of post rock and contains the fossil remains of the clam, coiled snail-like ammonites, and shark teeth.

Left: Duane and Damon Vonada, KS. Above: Stone fence post; Delmar Vonada breaking rock.

"They Want to Keep Their Rural Schools"

Verda Reisner teaches in District 27, a one-room school near Lewellen, Nebraska. In 1987 she had three students: Jon Jorgensen, a first-grader; Rochelle Meredith, a second- grader; and Erica Jording, a kindergartner.

Verda: The board is not too happy to [consolidate]. I really think it's great the way they want to keep their rural schools because they feel their children are getting a better education than they would in town. The children get more individual attention, and the teacher is more aware of what they are doing.

They took their achievement tests two weeks ago, and they all ranked as third- and fourth-graders. I was very pleased with them. Of course, Jon gets lots of help at home. His parents are very good to help him.

Jon: [I like this school] very much. All of us [get special attention]. You can sometimes interrupt classes.

Rochelle: [I went to school in Denver] all my life until I came here. [There are] all kinds [of kids], about five million.

Verda: I like the rural school. I wouldn't go into town for anything. I wouldn't put up with the guff that the teachers in town have to put up with. And I like this little location. It's so, I don't know, calm and serene. In the evening I just look at it—and it's just so quiet. We have trains, lots of trains going by, [so] you don't feel lonely out here.

I took them down to see the pelicans the other day [at Lake McConaughy]. One day . . . [we had] four kites flying. We had the papas and all of them out here trying to fly kites. We had a party for everyone Friday, and this Friday we're going to have a picnic with our track meet.

For Christmas, well, [the community] was all shocked last Christmas. . . . Rochelle left in October and went back to Denver. . . . The [community] was quite surprised that we had such a good program with two students. But [the students] did real well. They memorized everything. We just had a good time.

Lake McConaughy is a man-made reservoir along the North Platte River in Nebraska. The sandhill crane staging area is about 150 miles downstream near Kearney. Each spring nearly five hundred thousand sandhill cranes, four fifths of the continental population, pause here for four to six weeks before returning to their breeding grounds in Canada, Alaska, and the Soviet Union. Legally protected whooping cranes, five to nine million ducks and geese, 150 to 250 bald eagles, and thousands of other migratory birds use the Platte River valley and adjacent wetlands each year.

Left: Erica Jording, Rochelle Meredith, Jon Jorgensen, and teacher, Verda Reisner, NE. Above: District 27 schoolhouse.

"That Beautiful Steam Whistle"

Paulding, Ohio, school superintendent Stan Searing spends his vacations as a volunteer steam locomotive fireman for the Mid-Continent Railway Museum at North Freedom, Wisconsin. The museum features a working turn-of-the-century shortline railroad, complete with authentic depot, repair facility, and rolling stock.

"We have twenty-five hundred students ... [in] kindergarten through grade twelve. We just tore down an old 1884 building, the same age as our oldest engine here [at the museum].

"The love of steam engines is in my blood, and has been since I joined Mid-Continent back in about '62.... When I was in college I worked summers here. Mid-Continent is a not-for-profit historical society. Our purpose is to recreate shortline railroading from the late 1800's and early 1900's—no games, no fake Indian raids, just the real thing—with the original equipment.

"[We run] four times a day, May through September. We have a special snow-train run. I was here for that this year.... It was a blast. It's very exhausting to fire up a coal-fired engine [in] cold weather and keep the engines hot all night, [but it's] most enjoyable.

"It's great fun to see the old folks who had something to do with railroads come in and talk about how it was when they were young. You see the middle-aged guys, if I can count myself as that, bringing their young kids in, saying, 'This is the way it used to be.' The kids have wide eyes as they look at the fire and cover their ears for the whistle. To see a live steam engine, with all the sounds that it has, just five feet away is quite an experience.

"Railroads had a lot to do with [developing] the country. Of course, people went west before there were railroads, but to really get the crowds west, and to get the construction materials west, to be able to move goods back and forth, and the cattle—remember the old cattle drives—[it took the railroads].

"As the railroads went across the country they had enormous land tracts, government construction grants ..., and they were bringing people out to homestead on those land tracts, which, of course, created business for the railroads and created a profit for the owners....

"We chased a little deer this morning west of the track. First one I've ever seen.... We have four-and-a-half miles of track; a lot of it is uphill and downhill, with a tremendous number of curves. We head out from the depot and go up a hill along the old Baraboo River, which is just backwater now. After we crest the hill, we can see some of the Baraboo Range, hills as I understand it that were pushed up by the last glaciers that came down. And we head down past some of the old iron mines that were in the area. They've long since been closed. We stop at La Rue; workers from the iron mine lived there. Then we move on into the quarry that was operated until about 1960. We stop there at the quarry and allow people to get off the train and climb into the engine. They just love that...."

Engine No. 2 was built by the Baldwin Locomotive Works in 1912 for the Saginaw Timber Company. This engine burned oil to eliminate forest fires caused by hot cinders falling from the firebox. Many locomotives on long runs in the prairie states burned oil, because wood and coal were costly to transport. Mid-Continent restored engine No. 2 in 1982.

Railroads played an important role in development of the prairie states. Long distances and heavy cargo, difficult for wagons and pack-trains, were readily handled by the railroads. After the Civil War, rail traffic expanded rapidly until 1917, when it reached its zenith. The modern network of highways allows trucks to compete with the railroads for cargo, while airlines have virtually taken over the passenger business.

Left: Stan Searing, WI. Above: Stan and Engine No. 2.

"Well, there's always been poetry about steam engines that people who are gifted with the written word have done. [A steam engine] has a life of its own; they breathe. They're 'she's,' of course. They have to be treated carefully. I don't know if that's related to why they were called 'she's' many, many generations ago.

"I don't want to get maudlin and talk about, 'Oh, my goodness, I wish we had the steam engines back,' because it's not going to happen and I'm not going to try to make it happen. But I think it would be nice if some of our history courses would teach more about the evolving nature of things. Let the [students] make judgments whether it's good or bad.

"Whistling for the crossings with that beautiful steam whistle is something worthwhile saving for people."

Should Wisconsin be included in the list of prairie states? Over the years, prairie and forest boundaries have varied. John Muir talked of crossing a "miry prairie" from Milwaukee to Kingston in 1849. Aldo Leopold said that at times the forest retreated almost to Lake Superior, while at other times the forest reached south into Illinois. City names such as Prairie du Chien, Prairie du Sac, Pleasant Prairie, and Plainfield attest to the fact that prairie influence was strong.

Left: Wisconsin River, WI.
Above: La Rue Station, WI.

"The Early Hunters Killed the Mammoth"

At the Denver Museum of Natural History, Dr. Jane Day and her assistant, Cindy Wood, discuss the earliest inhabitants of the Americas.

Cindy: I discovered anthropology very early and had the opportunity to do field work. I just said, "This is it!" I knew it was the career I wanted to pursue.

Jane: I'm really what is known as a Mesoamerican archaeologist. I work in Mexico and in Costa Rica. . . . I think human beings have an eternal curiosity about who they are and where they came from. Anthropological and archaeological exhibits are popular because they give us all a chance to look at who we are and where we came from. Of course, you can always say we learn from the past, whether we really do or not.

Cindy: Many of our collections that relate to the plains and prairie were gathered during the Dust Bowl days when people were out walking in the fields and finding things exposed that had been buried for thousands of years. The 1930's is when people really got excited about archaeology out here, especially after the Folsom site finds.

The Folsom culture, the first evidence of it, was discovered in the twenties in New Mexico. Up until that time, it was thought that people had not been on the North American continent for more than two or three thousand years. . . . When the Folsom site was discovered . . . , when the points were found actually embedded in extinct bison ribs, they knew it had to be very ancient. It created quite a stir.

The earliest people we have evidence of in the plains and the prairie, and in North America in general, were the Clovis people. . . . They were mammoth hunters . . . . Big-game hunting adaptation implies sophisticated planning and group cooperation. They must have had an intimate knowledge of the environment and animal habits.

Jane: Meat was a major source of sustenance for these peoples. The front range of the Rocky Mountains, where the wonderful grasses grew, of course, made these herds possible. . . . [The early hunters] probably were very small bands, extended families, maybe anywhere from five to a dozen people. They slowly moved down [from the Bering Strait] all the way through to the tip of South America . . . . There were many migrations through time. Some are as recent as two thousand years ago, some as long ago as twelve thousand years; and people are still coming back and forth across those straits today."

Cindy: The early hunters of the plains hunted mammoth and the large species of now-extinct bison *antiquus.* . . . It's really unclear exactly how they went about hunting the mammoth. There is really no evidence, for instance, that they drove them into traps or that sort of thing. We suspect that they were using either a thrusting spear or a spear with a throwing stick, otherwise known as an atlatl.

Cindy Wood is the museum's assistant curator of archaeology, working primarily with North American archaeological collections. She has a master's degree in anthropology and museum studies.

Archaeological discoveries near Folsom and Clovis, New Mexico, where man-made spear points were associated with extinct animals, were the first evidence that human cultures existed in America as long as twelve thousand years ago. The Clovis people hunted the giant, elephant-like mammoth, but by the time of the Folsom culture the mammoth had become extinct.

Left: Cindy Wood, CO. Above: Cindy with mammoth skeleton, Denver Museum of Natural History, CO.

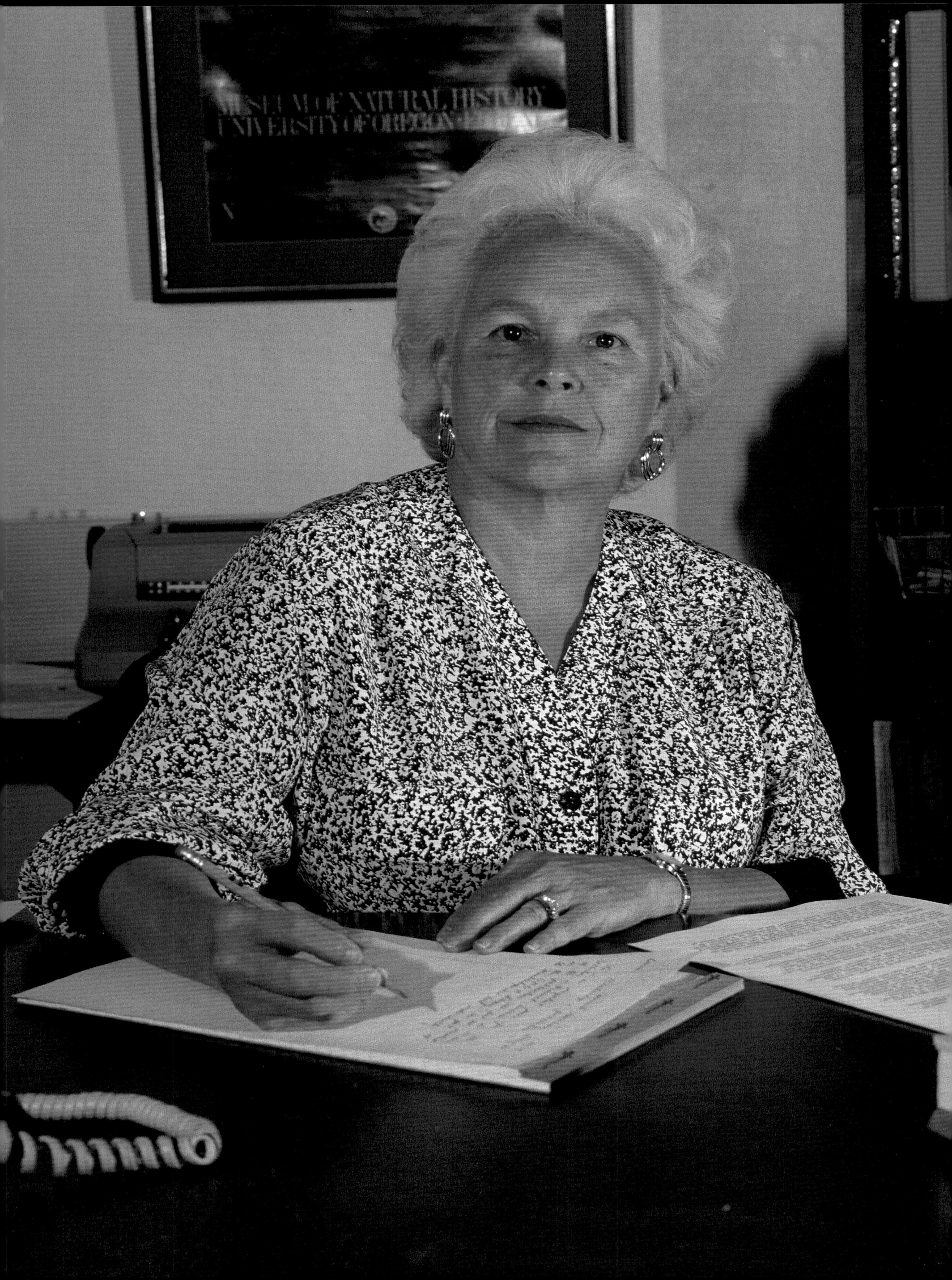
MUSEUM OF NATURAL HISTORY
UNIVERSITY OF OREGON

Jane: The great hunters of the New World followed the animal herds; they lived in what you might call a symbiotic relationship with these great herd animals. We have isolated ourselves from that because we no longer live in that relationship to the natural world. They were one with the creatures in their world. We do tend to think the world revolves around us in a different way. We have changed the environment for the benefit of human beings, if it indeed is a benefit.

[The human race] has learned that the more tools we create and the more cultural information we gather, the more control we have over the rest of our environment, which gives us a feeling of power. I think we're finding out today that we can't control everything.

I do wonder how much we've changed from the early people we're talking about. Physically, we haven't changed at all, and our mental capacity is still the same. One wonders how far we've come.

Dr. Jane Day is the chief curator of the Denver Museum of Natural History. Besides being the curator of archaeology, she oversees the areas of anthropology, zoology, paleontology, and geology.

Left: Dr. Jane Day, CO. Above: Tyrannosaurus skeleton, Denver Museum of Natural History, CO.; Cimarron River near Folsom, NM.

"I Saw Him Cry"

What follows is based on a conversation with an attractive woman at a cash register in a town of eight thousand. She speaks for many in the American heartland.

"Well, I like this town, but it seems like trouble just follows us. We moved here two years ago when we lost our farm. Now the town is hurting. It was bad enough, with the farmers and oil people not having much money to spend in town, but then they built a big mall on the edge of town, and, well, I guess you can see all the closed stores on Main Street.

"I liked it on the farm. Glenn was happy. He'd been a farmer all his life. Our little school for the kids was nice. Now, here they get into drugs and stuff.

"I remember when we got married, we were poor but we had each other and dreams. We went to a sale [auction] and bought a big oak table for our house. We had fun hauling it home in Glenn's old truck and talking about how we would fix it up and get some chairs. Glenn said when we got rich we would always keep that table.

"At first we farmed with Glenn's folks, then twelve years ago when they retired [in 1974] we had to buy the place. The bankers and Federal Land Bank loaned us all the money. They had charts showing how the prices of wheat would continue to go up . . . , so we signed on the dotted line. The interest was high. . . . They advised us it was okay.

"The first year was great: wheat went to almost five dollars. . . . Then Glenn bought the big tractor . . . and rented some more land.

"I scrimped and saved . . . , we had three children. I drove truck at harvest time and nursed the babies in the field. We worked all day and most of the night. . . . Then the grain embargo hit . . . , the Afghanistan thing, you know.

"We hung on a while. . . . Glenn changed, he was tired . . . , he didn't smile any more.

"The bankers got tough. . . . I didn't realize we'd mortgaged our house. Glenn took a job at night . . . , farmed on Sundays and whenever he was awake.

"We had to have a sale in January . . . bad time for a sale.

Auction sales are a social event in farm country. Usually held when a farmer retires, they often deal in generations of accumulated personal property and land. The anticipation of finding rare antiques and memorabilia attracts bargain-hunters and the curious. Farm families in financial distress, and creditors who have foreclosed on property, use the auction method also.

*Left: Old granary, IA.
Above: Catsteps in
Loess Hills, IA.*

"I was worried about Glenn, what he might do. The morning of the sale he got up real early and went out. . . . I was scared . . . ; I followed. All our stuff was lined up in rows.

"He got in the big tractor and just sat there . . . ; then he started crying . . . ; then he screamed and cursed . . . and prayed, screaming to God. I ran to the house . . . . He came in later, said it would be a nice day for a sale.

"It was hardest for me when they loaded the old oak table. Something inside of me went with it.

"The other Sunday, we drove into the country . . . and stopped near a fresh-plowed field. Glenn got out and felt the dirt with his hands a long time . . . ; for the first time since the sale, I saw him cry. He said he felt better then."

Trade with the U.S.S.R. brought the price of American grain up to record levels. Many farmers seeking to take advantage of the high grain prices borrowed money at inflated interest rates to buy land and machinery. The grain embargo imposed on the Soviet Union as a result of the 1979 invasion of Afghanistan lowered grain prices drastically.

Left: Harvesting milo at sunset. Above: Green antelopehorn bloom.

"This 'Greenhouse Effect' Thing"

John Lensch, a dairy farmer, lives in Marion, Iowa, and commutes to his farm near Alber-nette. He and his wife have two daughters, ages nine and six, and a boy, age three. He and two hired men milk about a hundred cows three times a day. They also grow eleven hundred acres of corn, soybeans, and alfalfa.

"This land is gently rolling, and so we have more creeks and that type of thing. I'm sure it was prairie land [originally]. There used to be a low area out in back, not really a swamp but a pond at certain times of the year. That's all been drained now.

"Marshes aren't real common in this area, but [my new farmland] down by the Cedar River has some marsh. It was kind of refreshing to farm a farm with cattails right nearby and little ducklings swimming. . . .

"Even in today's high level of technology the farmer is really subject to the weather for his livelihood. He's always been. You hear stories about farms that were dried out or burned out or [devoured by] swarms of locusts; you wonder why people didn't just let the locusts have it. . . .

"We try to set up our cash flows and projections and goals, just like any other business does, but one difference is, we don't create a product from a set of raw materials that we purchase; whereas if we're gonna make x number of pairs of shoes, we know that we need to purchase x number of square feet of leather. We don't know how much of the product we're going to have, and we can't set the selling price, so in those two areas, we really don't have a great deal of control. . . .

"I start at 5:30 in the morning, and at 5:30 at night I try real hard to quit. A lot of farmers farm at night. Grain farmers farm sixteen or eighteen hours a day, but then there's times of the year when they don't have to farm that hard. I work six days a week from 5:30 to 5:30, and on Sundays; I get every other Sunday off. . . .

"We do have some crop rotation. We use minimum tillage. All of my acres meet the requirements of the Soil Conservation Service's Food Security Act. . . .

"I think that there is a lot of room for improvement in this nitrate thing. We've just never really felt it was a problem until recently, and I think technology and farmers and soil conservationists will meet the challenge to find out more efficient uses of nitrogen in a way that it doesn't leak into the water system. You could simply say, well, we're gonna ban all chemicals, and you're gonna put half of the farmers out of business immediately. That doesn't mean that we might not be able to survive without them to a certain extent, but you have to find a happy medium.

During the ice age a cooling world climate produced a snow pack, up to two miles high in the north, which under compression forced huge glaciers as far south as southern Indiana. These glaciers gouged and pushed tremendous amounts of earth and rock ahead of them. Their staggering mass was large enough to carve out the Great Lakes. The water captured in the ice lowered the oceans three hundred feet.

The gently rolling, deep-soil fields of Iowa owe their origin to four glaciers that covered the land over a period of two million years. The last glacier, the Wiscon-sin, melted away only ten thousand years ago. The pulverized glacial debris, wind-deposited soils from the post-glacial period, and an ideal climate produced the luxuriant tallgrass prairies and the succeeding abun-dance of corn and soybeans. This ideal prairie environ-ment extends into Illinois, Indiana, and Ohio.

Left: John Lensch, IA.
Above: Martin Creek Farm, IA.

"I guess I still have enough faith in human ingenuity to be able to solve those problems. Now I don't believe enough in the human morality to think that we can do it before some serious damage might be done, but I do think that there will be. . . . People in this country are profit-oriented. . . .

"I think, in the last ten years, stewardship has become an important thing for us to consider. The United States was so large compared to the number of people. The people never felt that its bounty would ever run out. People have now begun to change their thinking, not only about the soil, but about the water, and about the atmosphere—this 'greenhouse effect' thing they continue to talk about. People are beginning to change their mind about the fact that this earth's bounty is infinite.

"I'm sure that land abuse and lack of business morals run out of the same vein. Somehow, we as a people need to look beyond next week. We need to even look beyond our own lives. A person's biggest goal in life is to make enough money so he can retire. That's a good goal, but yet the ultimate goal is to stand in front of God, and for Him to say, 'Well done, good and faithful servant.' That's where feelings of land stewardship come from; that's where business morals come from.

"We get so short-sighted in our thinking, the only thing we think about is: How am I gonna make that farm payment the first of March? Well, I can't say that's all bad because if we were just totally idealistic about it, we'd never make that farm payment in March. . . .

"Work is my enjoyment. I don't have any real hobbies. I enjoy singing, not professionally, but I like gospel music, church music, and I direct a church choir. But other than that, my kids are my enjoyment, and my wife; and the moments that we spend together, although somewhat limited, are important to me."

After the glacial ice had melted, exposed sediments in the Missouri River Valley were vulnerable to wind erosion. Great dust storms occurred, possibly lasting thousands of years. Resulting deposits of very fine soils up to two hundred feet thick formed the scenic Loess Hills of western Iowa. This soil, when eroded or excavated, stands in a vertical manner. Therefore the Loess Hills have weathered into an unusual terraced formation known as "catsteps."

Dairy cows must be milked two or three times a day, seven days a week. Milking three times a day increases production, relieves stress on the cow, and facilitates scheduling. In some dairies, cows wear transponders around their necks to automatically key computerized feed dispensers programmed to each individual cow. The computer also records milk production and animal health data.

Left: Typical Corn-Belt farm.
Above: Bufflehead ducks.

169

"Stairsteps from St. Louis to St. Paul"

Gary Clark is the lockmaster for Lock and Dam 22 on the Mississippi River near Saverton, Missouri.

"There are a lot of people that really don't know what the purpose of the lock dam is. [They] think it is for flood control. There's no flood control capabilities to it. These structures were built in the thirties strictly for navigation. Locks and dams are . . . a series of stairsteps from St. Louis to St. Paul.

"We lock canoes through here every summer. In the wall outside the gate and the same way on the upper end, there's a recess that has a rope hanging down in it. The [canoeist] pulls up there and pulls that rope, and it sets an alarm off here at the lockhouse, and we open the gates and let them through. They're taxpayers too, and this is their river too.

"A lot of people don't have any idea of the amount of commerce that passes through these places. In a year's time [it amounts to] about thirty-five to forty million tons. Grain, coal, and petroleum—in that order—are the three big ones, and then various other commodities. [One] tow [can be] sixteen barges—twelve hundred feet long and 105 feet wide—[loaded] about twenty-two thousand tons.

"[Navigating a river] is a little different than driving down a highway with a marked lane. . . . These guys are depending on their skill in the wheelhouse to guide that tow, and it takes several years for a pilot to be a good one. Years ago, the only way to get to be a pilot was to work on the deck and to get some captain or pilot to take you under his wing. Now they have what they call a master mate's and pilot's school. . . .

"It's more than just a job. You work out here several years, you get attached. . . .

"When we came back here, where my wife and I were from originally, we bought her grandparents' little farm over there [across the river in Illinois].

"We've got a camp five miles down the river. . . . When I leave here . . . and go home, soon as my wife gets home from work we may go to the camp and spend the night. . . . I've got a pontoon boat. . . .

"We fish and come up the river on the pontoon boat almost to the lock and float down the river and cook supper. [The catfish are] not as big as in the stories. I was a diver for the district here for seventeen years, and I worked around these locks. . . . I've never run into any as big as the stories."

A network of rivers drain the Prairie Bioregion and provide channels for river barges. The Mississippi, one of the largest rivers in the world, begins at Lake Itasca in Minnesota and flows into the Gulf of Mexico. It is 2,348 miles long and drains water from thirty-one states and two Canadian provinces. Thousands of rivers and streams flow into it. The Missouri River, by far the Mississippi's longest tributary, is 118 miles longer than the river into which it flows. Other major tributaries include the Ohio, Minnesota, St. Croix, Chippewa, Wisconsin, Rock, Illinois, White, Arkansas, Yazoo, and Red rivers.

The Mississippi, the back-bone of the inland waterway system, forms part of the Lakes-to-Gulf Waterway. Twenty-six locks and dams above the river's juncture with the Missouri help keep the channel open for navigation. The Missouri channel carries barge traffic as far north as Yankton, South Dakota, below Lewis and Clark Lake.

Left: Gary Clark, IL. Above: Tugboat and barge in lock; Mississippi bridge, Hannibal, MO.

"You Feel More Free"

Manuel S. Franco, an artist in Dumas, Texas, is a graduate of the University of Chihuahua with a degree in mining and metallurgical engineering. He specializes in Indian and Western art, bronze sculpture, portraiture, and wildlife. His work has been on display in various cities in Texas and in New York City for the last several years.

"I've been painting all my life. I started when I was five. I had the most beautiful childhood. We didn't have modern toys or anything but horses and a piece of land and cornfields and all that. Real nice. Real healthy. My mother used to take me out of the house every morning and wash my head and put me under this peach tree with a little table to draw pictures and do things . . . , you know, paint, print colors. . . .

"I do a little bit of everything. I photograph wildlife too. And I research a lot in magazines and books and stuff. And I volunteer for the Epilepsy Foundation because my little daughter . . . was born epileptic. I'm not the best artist. I have gone further than some. The friends around me—that's ninety percent of my success. . . .

"[I like the feeling] of being out in the open range and seeing [these plains just as they looked] a hundred years ago—no telephone poles and oil rigs or anything. Just nature. You feel more free . . . just watching those animals going by with no planes flying on top. . . . It's really nice. You [can almost see] a bunch of Indians traveling around on the horizon.

"[The Indians] were part of that land. They were born right there. Probably the same material. They came from the earth. They belonged there . . . just like a bird in the tree. . . . The Indian people . . . believed [the earth] was a spirit. . . .

"I've seen the bald eagle [at Lake Meredith]. Well, I'll feel sad [if they are gone]. We're not going to be able to see pronghorn around the city limits. We still see them once in a while. In this day we have to be productive, but we're using the land too much. Our resources are used too much, because the population is growing and everything goes faster and faster and the development of the land is going further. And one of these days it's going to pop. It has to have a limit. We have to come to preserve our resources—the water and the land and good management and all that, because we're going to need it. But in fifty more years we're going to have fifty million more people on this planet to feed, so we have to take care of our resources . . . , our water first."

The phrase "Six Flags over Texas" refers to the flags of the six nations in Texas history. At one time both the Spanish and the French claimed Texas. Mexico included Texas when it declared its independence from Spain. In 1836, Texas became a separate nation. Nine years later, it became the twenty-eighth U. S. state. During the Civil War, Texas was a member of the Confederacy.

The shortgrass prairie includes Montana, eastern Wyoming, eastern Colorado, western Kansas, the Oklahoma panhandle, northern Texas, and eastern New Mexico. Its western boundary is the Rocky Mountains. On the east, it ends at an irregular line of mixed-grass prairie from southwestern Texas to northeastern Montana.

Before European settlement of the panhandle of Texas, huge herds of antelope and bison roamed the area. "True" grassland animals populated it—prairie dogs, pronghorns, jack rabbits, and swift foxes. The burrowing owl, horned lark, killdeer, and mountain plover built nests in prairie-dog towns, and prairie rattlesnakes appropriated the burrows in the winter.

Left: Manuel S. Franco, TX. Above: Desert Christmas cactus.

"The People out Here Are Survivors"

Milton Cooper is superintendent of Quinter Schools. In May of 1987, he took his sixth-grade students on a field trip to Castle Rock near Quinter, Kansas.

"Our state ranks at the very, very top academically and educationally. There are not too many states that achieve better. In all the standard scores and the ACT's, the kids in Kansas rank consistently at the top. Education, of course, is expensive . . . because of the sparseness of the population out here.

"[This] is probably the greatest region in the United States: the healthiest, the purest, the cleanest. We still have decent water, and we still have air that you can breathe. We've got a good quality of people. We still have considerable morals and ethics. We care about each other a little bit more and perhaps cooperate a little more. . . .

"They're trying to make [Castle Rock] a state park—a state monument park. That way they can do a little better job of preserving it. It's gone down probably six or eight feet in the last four or five years. The tops have all gone down.

"Back in the Dust Bowl, you couldn't see some of these fences. The dust drifted like snow on top of them and you could walk over the top of [it]. It was a pretty desolate time . . . , and then it started raining and we had nothing but flood waters. There was nothing to hold it. All the vegetation was gone. I think [the yucca] survived the Dust Bowl times. It didn't seem to kill them, because they take a minimum of water. And of course your buffalo grass and your native grasses survived. But still they were all so short because of [lack of] moisture, so this was all dust out here.

"The yucca plants . . . are all over this part of the state. They grow out in the pastures. . . . The blossom is white, and when they all bloom it's a beautiful sight. They have a very sharp point. . . . A lot of people take them to their houses in town for decorative purposes. Certainly dogs don't come up and use them.

"People out here have had to survive under some pretty tough situations. The people out here are survivors. We've had the Dust Bowl and the blizzards and low prices. But these people are resilient, and they'll bounce back. They always have. They'll tough it out.

"[The people] are very optimistic. It'll be better next year. So they'll put that crop in or buy those cattle. They're just about as good a gambler as you find in Las Vegas."

The landmarks of Castle Rock and the Chalk Pyramids in Gove County, Kansas, consist of thick layers of chalk formed by microscopic plants and animals that lived in the last great sea that covered Kansas. Layer upon layer was formed as marine life died and filtered to the bottom creating chalk beds up to seven hundred feet thick. When the Rocky Mountains pushed out of the earth's surface, the Smoky Hill River began to sculpt the formations. Large fossils, some of them on display in the Smithsonian Institution in Washington, D. C., and in the Museum of Natural History in Denver, Colorado, have been found in these beds.

Left: Milton Cooper (center), sixth-grade students, and teachers, KS. Above: Students arrive, Castle Rock; Boys climbing rock.

"The Fish Weren't Biting"

Before his retirement, Louis W. Campbell was an engineer, a naturalist, and a newspaper columnist. Louis wrote an outdoor column for the Toledo Times *for thirty-four years. In 1988, at the age of eighty-nine, he was inducted into the Ohio Conservation Hall of Fame. He has been an advocate for preserving the Oak Openings, a pristine wildlife area, and is an avid bird watcher. He and his wife live in Toledo.*

"I saw canal boats myself, the last of the canal boats, when I was a kid. A canal is a big ditch about eighty feet wide . . . with a bank on each side for the barges to be towed. They would run a team of mules on one side and a rope hooked onto the boat, and they would tow the boat all the way from Cincinnati to Toledo. . . .

"I went into birds because, well, I was a fisherman and the fish weren't biting. I bought a pair of binoculars and I started to notice birds, and then in two or three years I found them very interesting. So, starting in 1926, I began to keep a permanent record of all of the birds that you see in the Toledo area. And I wrote my first book, *The Birds of Lucas County.* And this, believe it or not, was printed by the WPA.

"When I started out, there were comparatively few birders. Now they're running all over the place. There is a bird trail in the Irwin Prairie; ten thousand people a year visit that. . . .

"The prairie produces more birds, more different varieties of plants, more wildlife in general than the forest. A forest has very few bird species compared with the prairie. The prairie is the birthplace or the shelter place of a great many things in nature. . . . From the standpoint of studying things or introducing new plants into our gardens, the prairie is *the* place to work with. Nature did it. Nature follows the glacier with the prairie. . . .

"I go way back. I started [exploring] the Oak Openings around '27. So I've seen a lot of things happen . . . and big changes. And I've seen big mistakes made. . . .

"Now the Irwin Prairie [part of the Oak Openings] always did have swamp forest around one edge. When I first went there in the thirties, that place was completely [treeless] . . . ; and for years, that remained a prairie.

"The Drennan Ditch drained a good part of the Oak Openings and just destroyed them—beautiful land. Away from the prairies you had swamp forests and at intervals you'd get an area one hundred, perhaps two hundred feet in circumference, and there you'd get a lot of prairie stuff, wet prairie . . . with water in it up until July. And then, when they put in this drainage ditch, they completely drained it.

A band of yellow quartz sand dunes and scattered black oak trees near Toledo, Ohio, the Oak Openings stretch for twenty-five miles along what was once Lake Warren, the ice-age predecessor of Lake Erie. The lake was formed when the retreating Wisconsin Glacier deposited clay and rock and impounded its own melting ice. Later, sand from what is now Michigan was carried by wind and water to the lake's southern shore, forming dunes up to fifty feet high. The Oak Openings, prior to real-estate development, contained a grass-and-oak complex, wet prairies, and bogs, surrounded by a dense swamp forest of elm, ash, and maple.

Two Oak Openings remnants have been preserved by the Ohio Department of Natural Resources. The sixty-seven-acre Louis Campbell State Nature Preserve, named after the naturalist, contains the typical dunes with black oak trees, as well as poorly drained meadows with a diversity of bog and prairie plants. In the larger 142-acre Irwin Prairie, the landscape has changed since the surrounding swamps were drained. As water levels dropped, aspens and cottonwoods invaded the wet prairie to replace the sedge meadows. A fifty-acre tract of the original meadow remains.

Left: Louis W. Campbell, OH. Above: White egret.

"If you change the drainage system or dike the marshes you change the whole [ecosystem]; you change the habitat. Afterwards some people say, 'Don't touch nature. Let nature recover by itself'.... And I couldn't help but think, where have you been all these years? You simply *can not* do that. If you don't figure out [before you drain or dike] what you want you're going to end up with a forest. Nature works towards a forest. You can regulate a marsh just like a big garden. You can decide whether you want a lot of cattails, or whether you want, say, Indian grass. Nature responds very rapidly.

"They are building these great big beautiful houses . . . , and if there is a place where drainage can open it up for houses, that's what they're going to do. So, except for the Metro Parks, which will have to be controlled carefully, the [Oak Openings] is doomed.

"I am very pessimistic. Ultimately, man is just going to forget about conservation and so forth and just use up what he's got. Then, bingo!

"I don't think [people] will disappear. I think they may, like the Chinese do, start some very sharp methods of cutting down the population. That would be the first logical move. It could be a necessity. I was reading just the other day about the terrific amount of forest land that is being cut down in the Amazon and burnt off so they can have more land to raise food. So [population control] is a possibility."

In 1880, flocks of sandhill cranes nested in the Irwin Prairie area. Today, mallards, wood ducks, grebes, bitterns, rails, snipes, flycatchers, veeries, and many other birds nest there. Muskrats, minks, raccoons, skunks, opossums, red foxes, and white-tailed deer are some of the mammals inhabiting this prairie island. An endangered species, the spotted turtle occupies the wet meadows and shallow ditches.

The generic term "oak openings" refers to a transition zone between prairie and forest, especially in Wisconsin and Michigan. The bur oak is more tolerant of the prairie environment than are most trees, and hundreds of square miles of this hardy species once buffered the forest boundaries. The oaks' large canopies prevented the growth of forest underbrush and tall prairie grasses, and so park-like groves of oak and beautiful meadows greeted the pioneers as they came out of the dense forest into these "openings."

Left: Irwin Prairie, OH.
Above: Blue flag iris.

"An Indigo Bunting, It's Beautiful"

Douglas and Raylene Penner are restoring a one-hundred-year-old stone house on twenty-six acres of prairie as a weekend retreat, thirty miles from their home in Newton, Kansas. Raylene is a professor of English at Bethel College in North Newton, and Douglas is a psychologist for Prairie View Mental Health Center in Newton.

Douglas: We needed a place to get away . . . to compensate for what was pretty sedentary . . . and what we experienced as sometimes stressful times at work.

Raylene: I have a stone-house journal, which records when we spotted deer, and when the baby owls were [hatched], and when the butterflies migrated over. . . .

Douglas: There is a place about four miles from here where we often see something unusual when we drive through. One time we saw three young coyotes, maybe three- or four-month-old coyotes, cross the road. Another time we saw prairie chickens fly across the road, which is sort of rare.

Raylene: There's an indigo bunting two miles away from here underneath a bridge. It's a beautiful bird. . . . I've learned to appreciate birds now. [Being at the retreat awakens you to] all these things you want to learn because they're out here—trees, geology, rocks, birds, snakes. . . . We've become friends with the snakes.

Douglas: I think we saw an eastern racer or a yellowbelly racer. We watch the swallows. We've had swallows in the basement, and [we watch] the Eastern kingbirds. When we bought the house, all the windows were open and the Eastern kingbirds were nesting in the house, so we got to know them.

Raylene: [We have] no telephone. [A retreat] is a chance to absolutely forget everything you're doing and stop the hectic [pace]. [Another] thing we envision is fun "people happenings" out here. If we ever get it fixed up, it would be great fun to come out at Christmas [with] a bunch of friends [to] play in the snow.

Douglas: Listen to those sounds. There are things that I can't—I can't talk about. . . . The meadowlark sound is. . . . For me it's worth a whole lot just to hear that.

Raylene: We come out here and are sometimes very quiet and sit somewhere.

Douglas: And just listen . . . , just listening to bird sounds and quiet and some coyote sounds and things like that.

The greater prairie chicken inhabits undisturbed tall-grass prairies. It has been driven from much of its range by destruction of the prairies where it breeds. Breeding takes place after males perform fascinating courtship dances on communal grounds. The booming sounds they make during this courtship ritual can be heard more than a mile and a half away.

Some harmless prairie snakes are presumed dangerous. The yellowbelly racer makes a buzzing sound like the rattler's by vibrating its tail in dry vegetation. Though the racer may strike when threatened, it is not poisonous, as are the prairie rattlesnake and the Western rattlesnake. Rattlesnakes are more excitable and aggressive, while the racer may "play dead" if touched.

Left: Douglas and Raylene Penner, KS. Above: 100-year-old stone house; night hawk.

"Something in His Eyes, Wild and Free"

Annette White, an anthropology student, lives in Kanopolis, Kansas, in the Smoky Hills. Although not a native Kansan, she has an extensive interest in the state's early history and has worked to explore, clear, and maintain several historical sites. Two of these are Palmer's Cave and the manmade Faris Caves.

"[I maintain the caves] because I love this country. I love this land. I want to know every little detail [about it], not just the kind of rocks or the plants or the history, but everything—as a whole picture. . . .

"And I *love* a good mystery. When I discovered the catacombs [in Cave Hollow Park near Kanopolis], I felt exhilarated, like I'd found a new toy. I don't know how far back into the hill they go yet. That's the neatest part about it. The mysteries aren't going to be solved overnight. . . .

"When I came out [to the Faris Caves] five years ago, they were full of silt and the springs were stopped up. There was a jungle that had grown all the way into the entrance. I cleaned [the caves] out because they are a piece of art work. They are part of American history, not just Kansas history. . . . They're a monument to how man adjusted to and survived in an unpredictable environment.

"There is a perfect engineer's curve in the entrance of one of these caves, which was used as the springhouse. It was called the refrigerator room because the temperature never varied from sixty degrees in the room. Charles Griffey, the man who dug these caves, knew what he was doing. He did not use dynamite, but he chipped it out of the sixty-foot Dakota sandstone bluff with a chisel and pick. There are no support beams inside [the three] ten-by-ten-square rooms, which are about twelve feet tall at the highest point. . . .

"[I'm] 'associate caretaker' of the Faris Caves and of Palmer's Cave, [a natural cave] which is in Cave Hollow Park. [Palmer's Cave] is situated on an old Indian trail called the Pawnee Indian Trail. There are petroglyphs in [Palmer's Cave]. They tell a tale of the death of a great Indian chief. It's a fantastic story. John Dunbar, [a missionary], was shown abandoned villages—scattered settlements—along the north bank of the Smoky Hill River in 1832. I imagine the smallpox epidemic started hitting there around 1803 and that the Tapage Pawnee—if they weren't wiped out by smallpox epidemics—eventually merged with the Wichita and Republicaine. They disappeared on the Smoky Hill River and were probably the first tribe in the Caddoan linguistic family to become obsolete.

"I think [Palmer's Cave] was a holy place. The symbolism's there. The water's there—the water of life.

"There's a lot of [mysteries] out here. There's an 1878 photograph of the stone cairns; and A. M. Campbell, the founder of Salina, painted a picture of the landscape here in Ellsworth County, and in that painting stands a cairn. These cairns are nine feet around at the bottom, they taper up slightly, and they are about eight to nine feet tall. The mystery is that there is no documentation to those trail markers that I have found

The first white people to come into contact with Native Americans living west of the Mississippi River and north of New Mexico were the Spaniards. French explorers and traders, however, were responsible for naming a majority of the tribes. French names were given to the four divisions of the Pawnee tribe: the Loup, the Pahni Republicaine, the Pahni Piqued, and the Tapage.

The Pawnee Indian tribe is part of the Caddoan linguistic group. The Arikaras, the Caddos, and the Wichitas are also members of this stock. The Pawnees lived on the Kansas River in Kansas and the Platte and Republican rivers in Nebraska. Unlike many of the Plains tribes, the Caddoans did not adopt the nomadic plains culture but lived in permanent villages and practiced agriculture. The Mandans also lived in permanent dwellings.

Smallpox, cholera, measles, diphtheria, some influenzas, typhoid fever, and plague were some of the diseases that were introduced to the American natives almost as soon as the first explorers reached the North American continent in the early 1500's.

Left: Annette White, KS. Above: Petroglyphs, Palmer's Cave entrance.

besides the photograph and the painting. They're another one of those great mysteries. I'm glad I have the privilege and the opportunity to do what I'm doing now. . . .

"I've learned a lot about the animals and the plants around here. I was sitting by the little bridge [near the Faris Caves] and working—doing some writing and research—and I was real quiet. And all of a sudden I heard a clippity-clop on the wood planks and I looked up, and there was a ten-point buck just staring at me. There was something in his eyes, wild and free. It was something that everybody, every person wants. That made me content. That's my feeling about nature. And my part in it. . . .

"I feel that a big old tree has a soul or a spirit. It might not be the same kind of soul or spirit that we have, but it's got the living essence. [I think that] the Indians felt that way. They felt that the ground and the earth that you walk on not only sustained your life but they gave you the energy to live. They gave you the spirit and let you know that you were walking in the right path.

"Everything had a purpose [to the Indian]. Everything was in its own time and place, and [people] were guided by the things that they did and the circumstances around them. Sort of like, 'Go with the flow; [the energy] is taking me the right way, and I feel good about what I'm doing.'

"There's a sense of apathy in the world and a fear of the open, of the wild, unknown things. And when there's something out there in nature you don't know about, well, that scares some people half to death. I hope that most of the people that I've taken out [to the caves] don't feel uncomfortable very long. I hope that they go home with an understanding instead of a fear of things. . . .

"[I go] on top of the hills for inspiration. That's where the wind blows through my hair and that's where I can *feel* it. I can feel the wind. I can see all the land below me and I can—I don't know—I can feel it . . . in the hills. Here, I'm part of it—in the trees and stuff like that—but I can feel it up there."

Palmer's Cave and the Catacombs are two caves carved out of Dakota sandstone by natural forces in Ellsworth County, Kansas. Speleologists and spelunkers can find a variety of natural caves beneath the prairie grasslands.

Many trails crossed the area near Kanopolis, Kansas: the Pawnee Indian Trail; the Santa Fe Trail; a military trail connecting Forts Leavenworth, Riley, Ellsworth, Zarah, Larned, and Dodge; the Butterfield Stagecoach trail; and the Denver Trail, used as a short cut when gold was discovered in Colorado in the early 1860's. The explorer John C. Fremont, sometimes accompanied by Kit Carson, used the Smoky Hill Trail through the area on his expedition to California. Fort Harker was established in Kanopolis in 1867 to protect travelers.

Left: Sandstone.
Above: Ohio spiderwort.

"Folks Think It's a Giveaway Program"

"My name is Ted Hawn, and I'm District Conservationist at the Soil Conservation Service here in Lewistown, Montana. I'm thirty-eight years old. I've been with the SCS about twelve years. I'm in charge of Fergus and Petroleum counties. [Petroleum County has a] population of only about six hundred.... In fact, I think it's one of the most rural counties in the country.

"There are five different mountain ranges you can see from my house here. [Beyond] the Judith Mountains, off to our east, it's prairie from there until you get to the Appalachians....

"In a nutshell, my job is to try to promote conservation, to work with folks that could be from a small operating unit, city government, county government, to large ranch units; developing grazing systems . . . or strip cropping . . . or conservation tillage . . . or waterways.... It's real diverse in a county like this.

"CRP stands for the Conservation Reserve Program . . . , a simple land set-aside program. The objective is to take highly erodible land out of production for ten years.... And for doing that the operator gets a payment. We have eighty thousand to ninety thousand acres of the Conservation Reserve in these two counties. Wheat grasses are pretty much the predominant grasses being planted into [CRP land]. All are cool-season grasses, and then we'll often mix in some clover and alfalfa. They're soil-building plants.

"[The CRP] is a big investment for the operator.... He is responsible for getting a successful stand of grasses and legumes. There's controversy.... Some folks think it's a giveaway program. To me, it's a great way to get conservation on the land.... [Farmers and ranchers] cannot hay it or graze it or anything like that over a ten-year period, so if you're looking at it from a soil or resource standpoint, I'm not so sure you can do much better than that....

"I would hope [the public] would realize that the food they buy comes from the soil rather than the grocery shelf. We all have a stake in the soil out here, no matter who you are, whether you're a businessman or a photographer or a book writer or a conservationist or at the grocery store....

"Another part of the 1985 Farm Bill [we administer] is called the Food Security Act.... Anybody that's participating, farmer or rancher, in any of the USDA programs has to have a conservation plan on their place by 1990. The crux of the plan will be simply to get erosion to tolerable, sustainable levels on the land.

"The best-producing soils we have, with the highest organic matter, are in the top few inches. You lose those and eventually your production drops way down and . . . no food.

Ted Hawn and his wife, Kay, and daughters, Jessica and Julie, live on a high plateau with range land, farmland, and mountains all around sheltering mountain goats, mountain sheep, elk, mule deer, white-tailed deer, and black bear.

Soil loss the thickness of one dime over one acre represents five tons of earth. Not only is this eroded soil a loss to the farm, it creates problems such as silted ditches and reservoirs and high sediment loads for rivers.

Soil depth in the prairie states varies greatly. The Loess Hills of Iowa may have soils several hundred feet deep, while the range land of Montana and many other areas may have a soil depth of inches. Even deep soils suffer from erosion, because only the topsoil contains the humus necessary for food production.

Left: Ted and Kay Hawn with their girls, Julie and Jessica, MT. Above: View from Hawn home.

"People have the right to own the property, and private-property rights are very important in this whole thing. They also have a very strong responsibility, in my mind, to farm it in a way that is not depleting the [soil] out there. I hope we gain out of this an understanding and appreciation of that freedom. I hope the day doesn't come when they're being told exactly how to farm out there.

"There are areas in this county and in Petroleum County where I doubt if the country has changed much in a couple hundred years. You might have some change in composition out there of some of the plants, but in reality I don't think you'd see a dramatic change.

"I had several classes in college dealing with Aldo Leopold, father of wildlife management. Certainly, his ethic is very much a part of what I feel. I still feel that we can foster, through time, a conviction and a sense of appreciation toward nature and the land out here no matter what we're using it for, to raise livestock, wildlife, or crops, or whatever. To get people to appreciate that and to understand the various ecosystems is a very important part of what I feel my job is.

"I guess I enjoy my job and profession. I feel pretty lucky to be working in the soil-conservation profession. I feel I'm a conservationist on and off the job."

A complete prairie ecosystem is necessary to make topsoil, which develops from a complex process of plants, animals, worms, bacteria, and microbes stirring, decaying, and adding atmospheric nitrogen.

Left: Western wheatgrass. Above: Judith River, MT.

"Live a Little More Gently on the Earth"

Mary Beth Eberwein has a master's degree in life sciences from Indiana State University. A naturalist for the Terre Haute City Parks, she works at the Dobbs Park Nature Center, where a small butterfly garden has been established.

"Indiana is well known for its hardwoods. Besides oaks, there were a lot of beeches, sugar maples, hickories, elms, and then a variety of other trees, like sycamores. . . . North of Terre Haute, we have a remnant prairie called Little Bluestem Prairie. It was a sand prairie . . . on the edge of the Wabash River. And [twelve miles southeast of here] in southern Vigo County, there was an oak-hickory-prairie mosaic. As you drive along the country roads, you'll see prairie plants like big bluestem, prairie dock, and some of the other things. . . .

"In the prairie, you've got a lot of flowers producing nectar. Butterflies are nectar-drinkers. . . . I would think that the monarchs would really like the prairies because they're on their way to Mexico through here. And there are lots of open-space-type butterflies, like the black swallowtail, which would use the nectar.

"The black swallowtail especially likes to lay its eggs on Queen Anne's lace. That's not a native plant. . . . It's real hard to figure out how some of these plants got here. Like the dandelion came long, long ago with the Spaniards, apparently. A dandelion will not do well on the prairie. It likes it when people mow their grass because that gives it more light, more room. So we're propagating dandelions with our lawns. . . .

"We're hoping to initially start [our prairie] as sort of an ornamental thing—as an extension of our butterfly garden. We might have geometric-shaped flower beds where we put in prairie species. My brother, Paul, who has been collecting prairie plants and seeds for eight or nine years, is going to give us some plants like butterfly weed, rattlesnake master, and compass plant. . . .

"This is basically the only park in our city park system that is nature-oriented. It is very important to open the eyes of the children who come out here from inner-city Terre Haute. . . . I hope by . . . taking them through the woods . . . , we can help them to see that there's a lot more [variety in nature] than they knew about. . . .

"[My involvement with nature] has really changed my view of the world, because it has helped me to see how it's all interconnected. It changed my lifestyle in that I'm not nearly the throwaway person that I used to be. We are part of the world, even though so many of us don't feel like we are. Our ability to breathe has something to do with the tropical rain forests in South America putting off oxygen every day. I think if people start to realize that they can live a little more gently on the earth. . . . If we got away from a lot of our lawns and more into a natural sort of habitat around our houses, it'd be great for wildlife. Next door to the park we have subdivisions where the people are into completely green grass. In the spring, they bring in the chemical companies that are treating the grass to get rid of bugs and weeds. We don't know the long-term effects of these chemicals.

Some wildflowers now present along roadsides and in prairies are not indigenous or native but are mixtures of species from all over the world. Queen Anne's lace or wild carrot may be one of these. It is a member of the parsley family and an ancestor of the garden carrot. Its long root may be cooked and eaten. The common speedwell belongs to the snapdragon family and is native to the United States, the British Isles, Europe, and Asia. It was used at one time as a diuretic and an astringent.

A butterfly garden is a challenging and rewarding addition to any yard. Certain flowers attract certain butterflies. The eastern black swallowtail is attracted by parsley and carrot plants and by nectar sources such as phlox and milkweed. The host plants for the monarch are milkweeds and dogbane. The dwarf yellow or "dainty sulfur" feeds on weedy composites such as sneezeweed, bur marigold, and garden marigold, as well as chickweed (in the pink family).

Left: Mary Beth Eberwein, IN. Above: Monarch butterfly.

"Everything depends on everything else. For example, if we lose the monarch, we're not only going to lose some beauty, we might lose something else, [plant or animal], that might mean something to us in the long run. This is a very egocentric way to look at it because it implies that humans are the reason for the existence of the earth. I think God created us to be stewards of the earth, to appreciate it, to use it if we can, but not to wipe it all out. I think we can sort of change our 'throwaway' society. We can also change, [though it might not be] good for the economy of the United States, how materialistic we are. We can buy things that are going to last. . . .

"If you've got children, take them outside, even if [only into] your own back yard. Start showing them the things that are there: the ants, the beetles, the little tiny flowers that come up in the spring that we call weeds but that the pioneers brought with them because they were medicinal, like speedwell. Take them out in the parks and open their eyes to a broader world. Take them on nature hikes. . . .

"There are lots of people who aren't aware of what's around them and how important it is. [It's good] to find a stream with a log going across it, preferably, and to sit on the log and watch the stream and the things around it. Just sit there for a long time and have your eyes open to how much is actually there. After a while, you'll even see the little tiny creatures—the crustaceans and things—on the bottom of the stream, moving around. [Or] sit on a step for a while and just look around at the birds flying in the sky or the butterflies, or maybe the deer coming out of the woods. It's important to take time. You can even go to a weedy lot in the city and see an amazing diversity of things there in terms of insect life and plants."

Planting a prairie wild-flower garden can be as simple as raking a commercial collection of seeds into a prepared seed bed, regardless of whether they are native or indigenous; or as complex as finding a source of native seeds within a twenty-five-mile radius. Some plants, such as the spiderwort and wild indigo, may have different colors or shadings depending upon the soil and climate conditions in which they grow.

Recently more growers have become interested in the propagation of wildflowers, including native varieties, but finding these people may take some research. A few seed companies have begun to carry native wildflower seeds. Use caution when collecting existing seeds and plants. Some species, such as the San Rafael cactus, have become endangered with the help of collectors. In 1982, the National Wildflower Research Center was established on land donated by Lady Bird Johnson, a wildflower enthusiast.

Left: Painted lady butterfly. Above: Mary Beth Eberwein, IN.

Introduction: Reflections

When I reflect on the journeys Mil and I have made across the prairie, a flood of images come to mind, images nearly impossible to separate from an excursion to the Kansas Flint Hills in May of 1983. Although I have lived in or near this marvelous grassland area most of my life, that was a turning point for me, and an experience that I wish for everyone.

On that crisp prairie morning, hearing the coyote's last howl, the nighthawk's call, and the upland sandpiper's throaty whistle; watching the sunlight greet the dew-laden grass and illumine the wildflowers; smelling the rich earth beneath my feet; and tasting the gentle wind . . . I was transformed. I suddenly realized that, although I had enjoyed the prairie before, I had never perceived its essence. I had not before allowed myself to be touched. Now it stirred my consciousness and awakened something deep within me. I knew now why King David sought refuge and peace in the hills. I knew why Jesus meditated forty days in the wilderness, why Thoreau lived at Walden Pond, and why Aldo Leopold introduced his family to "second home" development on an abandoned farm.

What is nature's essence? I can speak only from my own experience and, being a member of the human race, I am influenced by thought, history, and my own impressions. For me, every encounter with the natural world brings renewal of the spirit, a fresh sense of kinship with the earth.

This morning I sat quietly before sunrise, enthralled by the call of a brown thrasher perched somewhere in a nearby tree. I listened intently to hear it repeat one of its hundreds of songs, and I hope to listen again and again until the melodies from this talented singer become as familiar to me as the meadowlark symphony. In that predawn hour, I wondered how many of the people we had met on our journeys were also listening—if not to the brown thrasher, to the nighthawk or the bluebird. Perhaps some were lucky enough to have seen the quick, shining flights of goldfinches that wintered earlier here in their drab attire.

The thrasher's was not the only voice. The calls of grackles, pheasants, quails, cardinals, blue jays, and robins filled the cool morning. I recalled a warm January day earlier this year when there had been no songs, and I had a glimpse of what spring would be like if birds such as the brown thrasher suffered the fate of the passenger pigeon.

What touches one touches all. There is among us a kinship with flowers and grass, sunsets and shining waters, the wind and flowering trees, the eagle and the coyote. The better I know nature, the more I sense eternity in humankind.

Carl Schmidt

Left: Spider web with morning dew.

The Mississippi Near Hannibal

The patriarch of rivers
    Curves through the continent's center,
        Sunders it,
Rushing rainwaters to the sea.

    The rhythms of time
        Tempt voyagers to gentle musings
            As his waters mimic
Neoteric show tunes.

    On the western side
        Relics of Little Dixie remain
            (The river cunningly waits
The call of new Cains and Abels).

        Along his banks, he harbors his majesty,
            Though dredged, locked, and dammed.
                Defiantly coiling and curling, he protects
        His marshes and pristine wild lands.

        Like a primeval monster sunning,
            His surface deceptively still,
                He can suddenly arch his back,
        Brutally reclaim history.

Severing islands
    From the restless currents of the world,
        The leviathan
Plays Dixieland to while his wait.

1850 to 1853

Voices vibrate in the bluffs of Mitchell Pass.
The Cenozoic strata amplify the sounds
With the buried remains of distant times.
Led from the east by the sandy banks of the Platte River,
The voices say, "We have passed the curious chimney rock,
The earthy sandstone, where we carved our names.
We are going to the promised land, to build Utopia.
It's a garden there—not unlike Eden.
We will prosper and grow rich there."

The bluffs loom high on either side.
"We have overcome the Great American Desert."
The wheels of covered wagons rumble
And from the protected bed empty eyes peer,
Intense and small, staring into space.
"The mountains are ahead," they blink
With the monotony, entering
The gateway to the Wild West.
"We can prosper and grow rich there."

From the summit breathes the voice
Of the Cheyenne, Arapahoe, and Sioux,
Its sound quiet and filled with fears,
Yet strong like the thunder of buffalo hooves.
Eyes seek black shadows running in the circle below
As the earth becomes wild—split
By the dusty snake of rumbling wheels.
The river runs red through tall green grass
Toward the gently rising sun.

Holocaust

*The Sand Creek Massacre site lies amid the soft, rolling
  lands of eastern Colorado,*
*Once unnamed by my ancestors, called Territorial Kansas
  before it became Territorial Colorado.*
*Beneath a cottonwood, the sacred rustling tree, in the Moon
  of the Changing Seasons,*
*I scooped up a hand of gravelly earth, searching the arid
  grasses for signs of lives lost.*
*My fingers sifted grains of sand for my primitive soul,
  murdered in the Moon of Falling Leaves.*
*At my back trailed a narrow road with a signboard proclaiming
  battle, not massacre,*
*Beside a post affording a locked, weathered, wooden donation
  box.*

*The Washita Massacre site lies in the red earth of western
  Oklahoma,*
*Once named Indian Territory for "as long as grass shall grow
  and rivers run."*
*In the Moon of the Snowblind, from a picnic knoll, my eyes
  followed the red winding river*
*Tied in place by green wheat ribbons. I found the bank where
  Chief Black Kettle,*
*The most peaceful of Cheyenne leaders, and his wife were
  killed in the Moon of Falling Leaves.*
*The scholarly debate continues, extolling and condemning, in
  turn, the hunter, Lieutenant Colonel Custer,*
*Evoking the Crusaders, Hitler, and Vietnam. My eyes
  were blinded by the high noon sun.*

(continued)

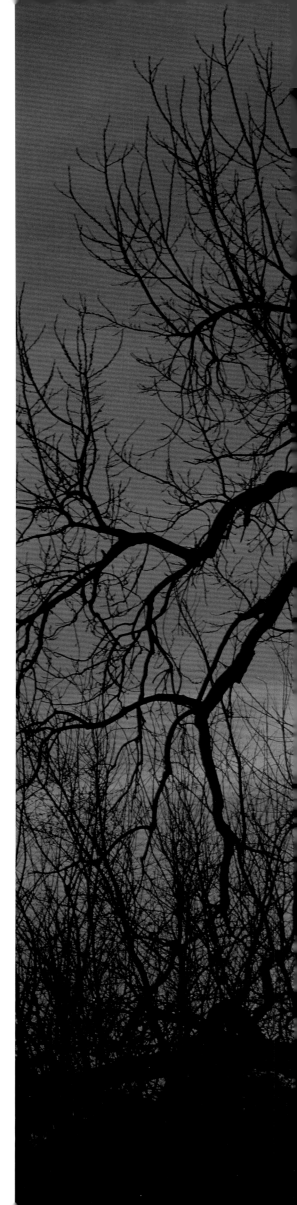

(continued)

The Battle of the Little Bighorn took place near the greasy
 grass in Montana.
Seven Moons of Falling Leaves passed before the rubbing
 out of long hair.
In the Moon When the Cherries Turn Black, my feet rested on Custer's
 Last Stand.
The Seventh Cavalry, vagrant immigrants, died in the Moon of
 Fatness.
In the shadow of the marble monument, naming the dead,
 marking the fallen,
A crude iron plate embraces the soil, joining Oglala,
 Cheyenne, and Minneconjous.
Brushed by the wind, my face bowed and led my eyes to the
 singing in the dark.

The Wounded Knee Massacre ravished the Pine Ridge
 Indian Reservation.
"A people's dream died there. It was a beautiful dream."
 said Black Elk.
I have not been where, in the Moon of the Popping Trees, the
 ghost dance ended,
Slaughtered by civilization, moralized by missionaries' "Will
 of God."
Breaking the hoop of the people sealed the conquest of the
 New World.
Now, in the Moon of Frost in the Teepee, I search the dream,
 the chanted rhythms,
Flowering histories of a quested world, civilized—yet
 still tribal.

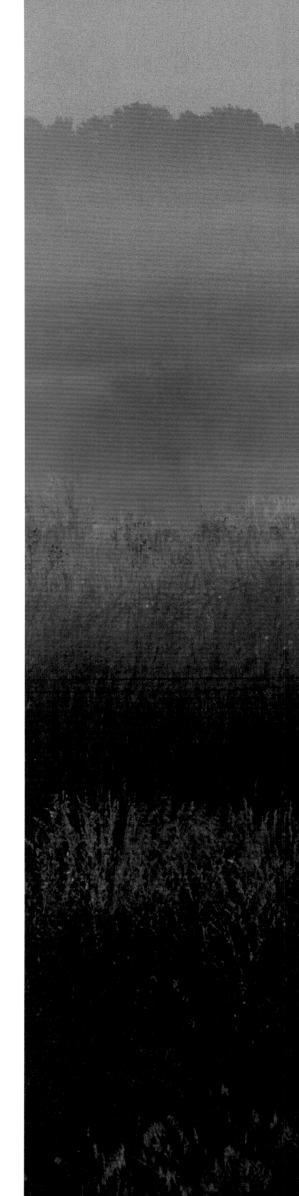

The Snowy Plover

A quick shadow blinks across the high sun,
  flutters north on the white sand:
Emmanuel, "God with us," a pale ghost bird,
  bears a black bar on its forecrown.

Badge-breasted, the plover darts to mother,
  her buff-and-speckled eggs
circled by rocks the size of a baby's fist,
  paled by the blazing afternoon sun.

The marsh rocks, cold and voiceless disciples
  of another existence, lie still.
The water grass to the south seems to murmur trust
  to the innocence of new life-to-be.

Brazenly, foolishly, the plover entrusts her eggs
  to this broad, flat, salt-marsh shore,
where eggs, twelve rods from a road leading east,
  cannot be distinguished from stones.

She does not know, twelve rods from a world turned harsh
  by thoughts of everlasting life,
one step could obliterate the golden promise
  of the snowy plover's destiny.

The Ballet

The pelicans, six—no—twenty at a time, are feeding.

Mutely they dance their ritual, synchronized

To the lap of wind-driven waves.

In white-feathered finery, they glide, heads high,

Their plumage trailing, soft chiffon waving,

Saluting the wind, their god of charity.

With mother love and selflessness, at the first beat

Of the flickering water great white wings direct

A shoal of young swimmers. The drum roll stops.

Open pouches bow in unison to fill swelling nets.

The primitive cadence rising again and again,

The throbbing, tuneless song ends. Appetites

Satisfied, the unseen conductor lowers his baton.

Catharsis

Early-morning darkness
paints cloud shadows
which shroud the tears
I have not shared
remembering my
unborn daughter.

Robins and hedge sparrows
wake,
calling me away
from their treasures,
the Wise Kings'
lapis lazuli.
The wind hums,
whispering
Egyptian secrets,
praising
the Mother's veiled shoulders.

From the wolf's den
eyes flare green
fire,
piercing wind currents
with a wild taste.
Darkness melts,
freeing the flower of nigella,
blue "love-in-a-mist,"
from its earthen sheath.

Will my daughter's eyes
know
wild indigo,
the blue cloud shadows
of her ancestors?

Requiem

In the mid 1700's, a flock of passenger pigeons might have been three or four miles long and a mile wide. Social animals, they flew so closely together that the sky and sun would be obscured.

Martha, the last living passenger pigeon, died alone in the Cincinnati, Ohio, zoo on September 1, 1914. Her body was immediately frozen in a block of ice and transported to the Smithsonian Institution in Washington, D. C.

In a relict prairie there is a eulogy the wind sings,
A reeded melody as fragile as the flowering switch grass.

Suddenly the sky darkens with the legendary roar of wings,
A moment's thunder, a flashing shadow, making the deer run
From the woven leaves of oak, chestnut, and hickory.

A plow with ripping blade stands poised in the void nearby,
Waiting like a ghoul to begin its greedy dirge.
One round stone stands, like a hard, cold sentinel,
Ready to mark the life in death beneath the earth.

Like Icarus, flying too near the sun, the ghostly wings
No longer breakfast on berries growing at nature's heart;
No longer feel the urge brought by the change of seasons.

Tall grass pendulates, passing time, in rhythmic phrases
While the mourning dove cries, a plaintive, low voice
Like a solitary flute played by the haunting wind,
Until I, too, dance like a brief shadow kissed by the sun.

Alone in a relict prairie I hear a eulogy the wind sings,
A reeded melody as fragile as the flowering switch grass.

The Bridge

Like vessels designed by Hermes,
    covered bridges invite voyagers
        to seek beyond rivers
That carry water to the sea.

Entry gives weary seekers
    protection, comfort from rain or sun
        to reminisce of childhood fancies
Rich with the warmth of wood.

Soon four corners beckon
    with strong directional beams
        binding together quarters,
Opposite sides of the passageway.

The canopy roof directs light beams
    from Sol and Luna, a crown
        like the flowering cow parsley
Delicately adorning the dark floor.

The wood creaks expectantly;
    footsteps echo to both ends
        from forest to the prairie sea;
Past and future joined by walking.

From the center, the traveler falters;
    windows open to the river below
        and halfway between east and west
The blue-white circles envelop him.

Encircled by friendship,
    transformed by Hermes' art,
        the seeker becomes the vessel
Carrying water to the sea.

Light

Fresh from the trauma of birth,
    hidden by its mother
        in a thicket
           of sumac and bluestem,
A fawn is betrayed
    by the sunlight's
        reflection
           in her eye.

She abandons her dark hiding place,
        bounds through thorny wild roses
        and over flint-
           speckled limestone
To stand, as if frozen,
    though breathing deeply,
        her sculpted back
           like dancing sunspots
Linking earth and sky.

At first, the brilliant daylight
    is blinding;
        and then the fawn's mirror eyes
           reflect the surroundings
Larger than life.

I lose myself in the mystery—
    the blackness of the fawn's eyes—
        and see creation:
           the nothing out of which
All may grow.

Sunset

The sun weaves gold

Through the land and its elements,

Into the prima materia *of earth.*

Arrows spin through cerulean blue,

Like threads from a craftsman's wheel

Into a wine colored solitaire

Fit for an emperor's crown.

A numinous time, light meets dark,

Weaving eons from hourglass sand,

Tailoring the greens and yellows

Of grass and flowers into a beryl sea.

Lavender threads of tranquility

Change the azure waters to copper,

And turn brown earth to red.

The love affair between dark and light,

Like an elixir of life,

Spins gold through cooling air.

Then the white moon rises

With the invincible blackness of night,

Turning coppery waters to gray,

And joyously abandoning the craft

In silvery laughter of dew.

Fantasia

The earth chants her dreams
in the timeless present,
exalts her fantasies in prairie rhythms
millenia old.

Her lightning illuminates the thunder,
embellishes the flowering trees.
Her breath recites her secrets,
enigmas to be heard in silence.

To the rhythm of darkness,
the great horned owl, night wizard,
flies mute as a moth from plain to tree
charting quarter points over the pathless land.

The lithe, gray, grizzled coyote,
fabled trickster of learning,
hidden on a hillock vantage,
croons his tales in the night darkness.

At daybreak, the owl and coyote vanish.

Weird wind whistles ascend.
Solitary, the prairie sandpiper rises
to the terrestrial rotation,
alighting with wings uplifted

On the silent breath of morning dew.
The messenger from pampas to prairies
awakens Aurora with
a liquid mournful cry.

The pristine monarch breaks the chrysalis
bound to the heart-protecting milkweed, and dries
its wings with sun-warmed breezes. This virtuoso
knows at conception the immanent phrases of life.

On the winds of morning, milkweed pods split
freeing silken-wrapped seeds.
The prairie hums incessantly, improvising
earthen dreams held in timeless darkness.

The Prairie Web

Inspired by a letter from Chief Seattle to the United States government, 1852.

The earth is sacred.
Every flower-blazed prairie
Covering gently rounded hills
Is sacred.

As the eagle watches the earth,
The rustling wild grain speaks for us.
Prairie bird songs float echoless
On the soft breeze—they are our songs.

> *We are born of the earth*
> *And taught by its nature.*

> *If we know the bear, the deer, the elk,*
> *The creatures of the earth,*
> *We know ourselves.*

> *As the prairie flower has*
> *Roots in the soil,*
> *We too have roots.*

> *The water that flows*
> *Is like the blood in our veins.*

Reflections in the shining waters
Speak of ancestral memories.
The murmuring streams
Tell us of our fathers and mothers.

The wind gave us our first breath
And receives our last sigh.
The spirit of life comes to our children
On the wings of the wind.

> *The earth does not belong to us.*
> *We belong to the earth.*
> *The fate of the earth is our fate.*

The web of life is not woven by us.
We are merely a strand in the web.
Whatever we do to the web
We do to ourselves.

> *Our life is brief*
> *Like the flight of an eagle.*
> *Our souls, delicate,*
> *Like the fragrance of a prairie flower.*

Brown, Lauren. *Grasslands.* New York: Knopf, 1984.

Campbell, Joseph. *The Power of Myth.* New York: Doubleday, 1988.

Collins, Joseph T., ed. *Natural Kansas.* Lawrence, Kansas: University Press of Kansas, 1985.

Cooper, Tom C., exec. ed. *Iowa's Natural Heritage.* Des Moines, Iowa: Iowa Natural Heritage Foundation and the Iowa Academy of Science, 1982.

DeMallie, Raymond J., ed. *The Sixth Grandfather: Black Elk's Teachings Given to John G. Neihardt.* Lincoln and London: University of Nebraska Press, 1984.

Devall, Bill and George Sessions. *Deep Ecology.* Layton, Utah: Gibbs M. Smith, 1985.

Diekelman, John and Robert Schuster. *Natural Landscaping: Designing with Native Plant Communities.* New York: McGraw-Hill, 1982.

Elman, Robert. *First In the Field: America's Pioneering Naturalists.* New York: Van Nostrand Reinhold, 1977.

Evans, Terry. *Prairie: Images of Ground and Sky.* Lawrence, Kansas: University Press of Kansas, 1986.

Gard, Robert E. *Coming Home to Wisconsin.* Madison: Stanton and Lee, 1982.

Gleick, James. *Chaos: Making A New Science.* New York: Penguin Books, 1987.

Gould, Stephen Jay. *Time's Arrow Time's Cycle.* Cambridge, Massachusetts: Harvard University Press, 1987.

Halpern, Daniel, ed. *On Nature: Nature, Landscape, and Natural History.* San Francisco: North Point Press, 1987.

Jackson, Wes. *Altars of Unhewn Stone.* San Francisco: North Point Press, 1987.

Johnson, Lady Bird and Carlton B. Lees. *Wildflowers Across America.* New York: Abbeville Press, 1988.

Leopold, Aldo. *A Sand County Almanac.* New York: Oxford University Press, 1949.

Little, Elbert L. *The Audubon Society Field Guide to North American Trees: Eastern Region.* New York: Knopf, 1980.

Little, Elbert L. *The Audubon Society Field Guide to North American Trees: Western Region.* New York: Knopf, 1980.

Madson, John. *Where the Sky Began: Land of the Tallgrass Prairie.* San Francisco: Sierra Club, 1982.

Meine, Curt. *Aldo Leopold: His Life and Work.* Madison: University of Wisconsin Press, 1988.

Muir, John. *The Story of My Boyhood and Youth.* Layton, Utah: Gibbs M. Smith, 1980.

Niering, William A. *The Audubon Society Field Guide to North American Wildflowers: Eastern Region.* New York: Knopf, 1979.

Niering, William A. *Wetlands.* New York: Knopf, 1985.

Peterson, Roger Tory. *A Field Guide to the Birds East of the Rockies.* Boston: Houghton Mifflin, 1980.

Pyle, Robert Michael. *The Audubon Society Field Guide to North American Butterflies.* New York: Knopf, 1981.

Spellenberg, Richard. *The Audubon Society Field Guide to North American Wildflowers: Western Region.* New York: Knopf, 1979.

Thompson, Ida. *The Audubon Society Field Guide to North American Fossils.* New York: Knopf, 1981.

Thoreau, Henry David. *The Natural History Essays.* Layton, Utah: Gibbs M. Smith, 1980.

Thornton, Russell. *American Indian Holocaust and Survival: A Population History Since 1492.* Norman and London: University of Oklahoma Press, 1987.

Trimble, Stephen, ed. *Words From the Land: Encounters with Natural History Writing.* Layton, Utah: Gibbs M. Smith, 1988.

Unruh, John D. *The Plains Across: The Overland Emigrants and the Trans-Mississippi West, 1840–60.* Urbana, Illinois: University of Illinois Press, 1979.

Van Bruggen, Theodore. *Wildflowers, Grasses, and Other Plants of the Northern Plains and Black Hills.* Interior, S.D.: Badlands Natural History Association, 1971.

Whitaker, John O. *The Audubon Society Field Guide to North American Mammals.* New York: Knopf, 1980.

Worster, Donald. *Dust Bowl: The Southern Plains in the 1930's.* Oxford: Oxford University Press, 1979.

Bold page numbers indicate photographs